PARENTS MATTER:
Supporting the Birth
to Three Matters
Framework

Edited by Lesley Abbott and Ann Langston

Open University Press

Open University Press
McGraw-Hill Education
McGraw-Hill House
Shoppenhangers Road
Maidenhead
Berkshire
England
SL6 2QL

email: enquiries@openup.co.uk
world wide web: www.openup.co.uk

and Two Penn Plaza, New York, NY 10121–2289, USA

First published 2006

A catalogue record of this book is available from the British Library

ISBN-10: 0335 21980 2 (pb) 0335 21981 0 (hb)
ISBN-13: 978 0335 21980 3 (pb) 978 0335 21981 0 (hb)

Library of Congress Cataloguing-in-Publication Data
CIP data applied for

Typeset by YHT Ltd, London
Printed in Poland by OZGraf S.A.
www.polskabook.pl

Contents

List of Contributors

Lesley Abbott is Professor of Early Childhood Education at the Manchester Metropolitan University. She directed the *Birth to Three Matters* project for the DfES and Birth to Three Training Matters funded by the Esmeé Fairbarn Trust. She has published widely in the field and has worked as a consultant in Australia, Singapore and Ireland.

Caroline Barratt-Pugh is a Senior Lecturer in Early Childhood Education (0–8 years) at Edith Cowan University in Western Australia. She teaches postgraduates and undergraduates, and is involved in the development of a new 'Birth to 8 Years' BA. She is currently director of the evaluation of the Better Beginnings: Books for Babies initiative in Western Australia.

Clare Crowther was, until her recent maternity leave, Senior Educator at Bridgwater Early Years Centre, Somerset, responsible for children under 3. Her chapter focuses on her daughter Eve, and the journey she and her husband, Steve, made as they became new parents. Before Eve's birth she worked extensively with parents to support them in using the *Birth to Three Matters* framework and materials.

Tricia David is Emeritus Professor of Education at Canterbury Christ Church University College. Formerly Professor of Education at Canterbury Christ Church University College, Tricia's research and writing is mainly concerned with the earliest years. Her publications include 15 books and over 70 journal articles and book chapters. Tricia has recent first-hand experience of being a grandparent of young children, in whose lives she plays an important role.

Ann Farrell is Associate Professor in the School of Early Childhood and Co-Leader of the Early Years Research programme at Queensland University of Technology. Ann is Chief Investigator in a range of research projects. She has written a wide range of book chapters and journal articles in the areas of children and the law, policy research, early childhood education, family studies and criminology.

Margaret Henry has been a researcher, at the University of Queensland and Education Queensland, in projects concerned with early development, the support of children with special needs, childcare and collaboration with indigenous families. Now retired, she continues to collaborate with QUT colleagues in research on everyday activities and learning. She has always been interested not only in how adults can help children to develop, but in how we can also help one another's development.

Rachel Holmes is a Research Associate and Senior Lecturer at the Manchester Metropolitan University. She recently directed a partnership project with Manchester City Art Gallery into the experiences of families with young children accessing museums and art galleries. Her research and teaching interests include children's rights, the individual and the social in childhood, constructions of early childhood and engaging families in their children's learning. She is currently studying for a Ph.D.

Kim Holyman is the Care Manager for under 3s provision and family support at Tamworth Early Years Centre in Staffordshire. The centre provides integrated care and education for children aged 1 to 5 and support for their families. Earlier in her career she worked in social services day nurseries as a nursery nurse and manager. She recently completed her BA in Early Childhood Studies.

Elizabeth Howard is the Health Lead for a Sure Start programme where she supports and initiates contact with parents and carers of children 0–4 years of age and expectant mothers, and is involved with strategies for health development. She spent many years teaching trainee nursery nurses in health, childcare and development, and psychology. Recently she returned to the field of health visiting and this led to her present role.

Julie Jennings is a trained teacher who has specialized in the care and education of children with special educational needs and disabilities. As Early Years Development Officer, she is taking the lead in promoting services which will improve the range and quality of early childhood provision for children with a visual impairment from birth to 5 years, and their families. She has recently been elected chair of the national Early Childhood Forum.

Ann Langston is an early education consultant, writer and researcher, based at Manchester Metropolitan University. With a background in advisory work in an LEA, teacher education and nursery nurse education she has managed under 5s provision in an early years service. A major contributor to the development of the *Birth to Three Matters* framework and the *Birth to Three Matters* childcare workforce materials she also managed the Sure Start/DfES *Birth to Three Matters* training programme.

Alison Lockley trained and worked in youth and community development before working for ten years in supported housing, providing accommodation for single homeless people with a variety of support needs. Alison has conducted research into the impact of social exclusion upon teenage mothers' aspirations towards, and access to, further education and additionally a comparative study of US and UK welfare benefit systems with specific regard to their support for lone parents.

Helen Moylett works for the DfES as a Senior Regional Adviser for the Foundation Stage. Prior to that she was Head of Tamworth Early Years Centre in Staffordshire. Earlier in her career she worked as a senior lecturer in education studies. She has also been a home-school liaison teacher in inner-city Manchester. She has co-edited three books with Lesley Abbott and was a member of the steering group for the *Birth to Three Matters* framework.

Sue Owen is Director of the Early Childhood Unit at the National Children's Bureau. Previously Sue was Early Years Development Officer for Humberside County Council with a brief to coordinate and develop services across the statutory, voluntary and private sectors and with local communities and parents' organizations. As part of her work for the Early Childhood Unit Sue has been chairing the panel for Investors in Children, the government's early years quality assurance endorsement scheme. Sue is currently completing a doctorate on the development of organized systems of childminding.

Stephanie Petrie is a Senior Social Worker at the University of Liverpool. She is currently an external examiner for Reading University and co-trustee of a young person's criminal injuries compensation trust fund. Her research interests are in the developing mixed economy of welfare as it affects services for children and their families, particularly children's daycare. She recently completed a two-year study, funded by the Teenage Pregnancy Unit (DfES), together with colleagues from several universities.

John Powell is Senior Lecturer and Multi-Professional Coordinator in Early Childhood Studies at the Institute of Education at Manchester Metropolitan University with particular interests in child protection, equal opportunities, children's rights, multi-professional perspectives, professional development and research. He is also involved in teaching across a range of levels and subjects relating to childcare and childcare practices. He has produced articles and chapters for publications and contributed widely to international conferences.

Mary Rohl is a Senior Lecturer in the School of Education at Edith Cowan University in Perth, Western Australia. She has had many years' experience as an early childhood professional: in the UK she was a playgroup leader and taught in nursery and infant schools. She is co-director with Caroline Barratt-Pugh of the Better Beginnings family literacy programme in Western Australia.

Collette Tayler is Professor and Head of the School of Early Childhood at Queensland University of Technology. She is Chief Investigator with Ann Farrell in the ACCESS Study of Child and Family Services in Rural and Disadvantaged Communities (2000–2) and the Australian Research Council-funded Impact Study of Child and Family Hubs. She has published extensively in the areas of early literacy, early childhood curriculum and policy.

Lee Tennent is a Senior Researcher in the Centre for Learning Innovation at Queensland University of Technology. She has been a researcher in major projects with young children and their families in rural and remote communities and in state-wide evaluation of a preparatory year for some 2000 young children in Queensland schools. She has authored many scholarly publications and presented her work to numerous international conferences in early childhood education and care.

Preface

Anybody who works young children usually also works with their parents – and people who work with the youngest children tend to work even more closely with parents, because they are the most important people in young children's lives. The idea for this book arose from many discussions with practitioners who, having enthusiastically embraced the principles in the *Birth to Three Matters* framework, and having read with equal enthusiasm our book, *Birth to Three Matters: Supporting the Framework of Effective Practice*, identified that partnership with parents was an important facet of their work, and an area where learning often took place in the workplace. This book, which emerged from these discussions is offered in support of practitioners in settings as disparate as crèches and children's centres. It is intended to provoke their thinking, inform their practice and challenge their assumptions. In the first chapter, Why Parents Matter by Ann Langston, we consider the issues parents and practitioners face in the context of constantly expanding childcare provision, the pressure on parents of working and caring for their children and how, if children are to have the best of both their worlds – that is, their home life and their lives in daycare, parents and practitioners must work together. In Chapter 2, Becoming a Family, Clare Crowther describes the journey taken as her family increased when her daughter was born and the joys, adjustments and choices that were made following this event. Chapter 3 by Tricia David takes up some of the issues that were important in Clare's journey and points to the powerful role of grandparents in the lives of their children and their children's children – the legacies of 'narratives of their own attachments' that are passed on through generations, predicting warmth and responsiveness of new parents to their newborn infants. Still looking at the roles of adults in children's lives and building on from the idea of a 'secure base', Margaret Henry, in Chapter 4, explores the ways in which, through activities with their children, parents can be helped to fulfil their own needs at the same time as meeting their children's needs. Moving from the home to a broader context in Chapter 5 Helen Moylett and Kim Holyman consider how, even when there is potential conflict between the needs and interests of children and their parents, skilled practitioners can manage relationships that rely on honest, open communication and which maintain support for both parents and children at difficult times. The same theme is revisited by John Powell in Chapter 6, Parents and Child Protection Matter, when we are reminded that child protection may need to be extended to parents. In Chapter

7, Caroline Barratt-Pugh and Mary Rohl describe the processes involved in working with parents to develop skilful communicators and competent learners through sharing books, rhymes and songs. Reflecting that work in this country mirrors much of what occurs in the southern hemisphere, Chapter 8, by Elizabeth Howard, explores the nature of support in a Sure Start programme led by a primary care trust, where health matters are addressed in positive and supportive ways that empower parents. In Chapter 9, in a very different out of home context, Rachel Holmes discusses the tensions professionals face as they explore 'Arty-farty nonsense' in an art gallery with parents and young children, recognizing that principles and practice are often compromised as, through relationships, power is negotiated and rules established. Moving on to consider families whose children have special needs or disabilities, in Chapter 10 Julie Jennings explores the complex and sometimes challenging view that 'parents should be viewed as experts on their child, equivalent and complementary to those who have other expertise to offer'. The thesis for this chapter is the core of effective work with parents and is echoed in the chapters that follow. In Chapter 11 Sue Owen and Stephanie Petrie outline the emphasis placed by the educationist Magda Gerber on relationship-based parent education that is founded on close observation of the child, and this is reiterated in Chapters 13 and 14 with reference to parents. The final chapter by Lesley Abbott, Future Matters, brings together many of the issues pertaining to work with parents and young children in the years ahead – it is a long journey and there is likely to be much change in the way we work with children and their families. We look forward to the future with hope.

Acknowledgements

We are grateful to the many contributors who have shared with us their knowledge, experience and practice both directly and indirectly throughout this book. We have acknowledged many times that working with young children is both complex and demanding. Each chapter demonstrates that this statement is equally true when working in partnership with their parents.

Practitioners working with children from birth to 3 and their families share both the privilege and the responsibility attached to working with the family unit at this most important time in their lives. We hope that this book will support as well as challenge all those who are involved in this work. Our thanks are due to all these people and to Angela Kerr and Michelle Huntington at Manchester Metropolitan University for their advice, support and skill in producing the manuscript.

1 Why Parents Matter

Ann Langston

In this chapter I will consider the significance of parents[1] in their children's lives, particularly of the youngest children aged from birth to the start of schooling at 5 years of age. Following the passage of the Human Rights Act, Jack Straw, British Foreign Secretary, was quoted as saying 'Parenting is hugely important to creating the kind of society we want to live in', arguably because 'it, [the quality of parenting] has a public face. It impacts on child outcomes and well-being, and consequently has deep-seated implications for society' (Henricson 2003: 1–2). Hence, the government's interest in parents getting parenting right. Parenting can be difficult though, for some people, especially those who have few role models. Little or no training is available for 'new' parents whose only mentors are often their own parents, and with such limited preparation it is easy to empathize with a new mother who explained her uncertainty about how to care for her newborn daughter with the words: 'I've never been a parent before'.

A major concern for governments and indeed the majority of citizens is the maintenance of social order through the glue of social capital, and organizations, such as the World Bank, state that 'increasing evidence shows that social cohesion is critical for societies to prosper economically and for development to be sustainable' (World Bank 1999). Social capital is defined as 'connections among individuals, social networks and the norms of reciprocity and trustworthiness that arise from them' (Putnam 2000: 19). It can be argued that at micro level families are the places where society either accrues or wastes such a 'commodity'. Thus if the family unit, however it is constructed (and this is a discussion I shall address only briefly) reaches out successfully to others 'to form friendships and supportive neighbourhood networks' (Sutton and Murray 2004: 29) then social capital increases, while if the family unit is under stress, and living in a disorganized high-crime neighbourhood, social capital leaks out like water through a hole in a bucket. It is to this end that the government wishes to 'reduce risk factors and increase protective factors by offering sustained support to parents of very young children' (Sutton and Murray 2004: 29).

Perhaps surprisingly, one period which is most stressful for parents is

---

[1] The word parents is used to refer to mothers, fathers, legal guardians and the primary carers of children in public care (Sure Start).

during a pregnancy and in the first years following the birth of a child. This contrasts strongly with the blissful view of parenthood portrayed in much of the popular press. We know, for example, that many new parents struggle with things such as tiredness, with as many as one in five mothers and one in four fathers who were woken up more than once a night by their babies reporting lack of sleep to be the 'most difficult thing about being a parent' (www.esrcsocietytoday.ac.uk). Balancing work and family life and financial issues also play a part in straining relationships as parents adjust to their new roles. Ironically, these factors do not simply affect their own relationship since it is also known that the 'way parents manage their relationship as a couple can have an impact on child development' (Page 2002: 2). So, at a time when media messages convey that life is, or should be wonderful, many new parents often find that their emotional and physical resources are drained and unless they have a wider support network the relationship which brought about the birth of the child is often strained and/or broken, leaving both them and their children vulnerable to psychological, economic and other stressors, the negative impact of which is inestimable. The same is also true, of course, for all new parents, regardless of whether they are the child's birth parents, including lone parents and single-sex parents. Similarly, many parents of children with particular needs experience these difficulties, which are often compounded by the additional issues surrounding their child's condition. A group who often remain 'unseen' are parents whose child has died at, or around, birth. Whatever the particular circumstances, it is at times such as these that parents often need most help, and practitioners in childcare settings may be the source of such support, particularly in areas where children's centres have been, or are being, established.

In the past, relationships between practitioners in early years settings and parents of very young children focused initially on a two-way transmission of information about the child and their admission to, and settling in to, the setting. In childcare settings information exchange largely related, where babies were concerned, to the child's responses to their new carers, their general health and well-being, and issues such as food intake, sleep patterns and bladder and bowel movements. This, to some extent, mirrored the model in schools, where involvement between parents and practitioners tended to occur most frequently when the child first entered the setting, lessening as they settled in as a pupil; though the progress of the latter might occasionally be punctuated when something significant occurred, such as a child being taken ill, or where concerns about behaviour or learning were identified. Later, however, this approach was superseded by a wider involvement, when non-working parents were invited to contribute to the setting (and hence their child's experiences within it) by undertaking tasks such as accompanying groups on trips out, or developing materials. Again, this was similar to what happened in schools, though over time, with increasing recognition of the value of involving parents in their child's care and education, practitioners began to expand their traditional roles by, for example, making visits to children's homes in order to create an early relationship with the family before the child began to attend the setting.

Subsequently, the extension of parental involvement, or participation, extended into wider programmes involving the transmission of skills and knowledge, and parents' involvement in the day-to-day events of the setting became the norm. Increasingly this led, some would argue, to an equal partnership between educators and parents, as parents were encouraged to become involved as trainees in a setting, or to contribute to the management of it – as a governor or committee member. So, the role of parents in early years settings has evolved significantly and increasing knowledge about the valuable role parents play in their children's lives has led to an emphasis, by the government, on involving them as much as possible in order to enhance outcomes for children's development. Indeed it has been demonstrated that even the smallest amount of involvement can be helpful. In one study of an intervention to support relationships between newborns and their parents,15-minute massage sessions by fathers of their young babies were found to enhance father/child relationships 'to the extent that the infants displayed more warmth and enjoyment during floor play interactions by the end of the study period' (David *et al.* 2003: 63).

Family life and the ways families are constructed in Britain changed during the twentieth century as 'Families became smaller as the birth rate fell and women married, then had children at a later age ... more single parents established their own households. More couples lived together, or divorced and remarried' (NFPI 2003: 1). The consequences for parents and children of this trend were that many family groups were re-constituted with 'little information about the numbers of children growing up in "unofficial" stepfamilies (where neither partner is remarried or cohabiting full-time) or in part-time stepfamilies (where children spend time with both parents in turn) in gay families or in families where parents are each from a different religion or culture' (NFPI 2003: 3). While 'official' stepfamilies account for only 8 per cent of families with dependent children, what is known about single parents is that there are an estimated 1.75 million with resident children – about one quarter of families; and of these, 88 per cent are headed by lone females. Indeed, in asking 'who is a parent?' a recent report argued that 'From legislation to parenting literature, the term "parent" might be used but it was largely interchangeable with the word "mother"' (Henricson 2003: 57). So, particularly where babies and very young children are involved, mothers frequently take greater responsibility than men in caring for them, and they often do so in difficult circumstances. A related issue facing many parents as the government encourages them to join the labour market is that they 'are facing the difficult task of juggling the responsibility of being a good parent with holding down a job' (Henricson 2003: 27) and, in families headed by a lone parent, the juggling is even more complex.

As indicated by heavy government investment in initiatives such as the Sure Start programme, and the measures set out in the *Five Year Strategy for Children and Learners* (DfES 2004) and in *Choice For Parents, the Best Start for Children: a Ten Year Strategy for Childcare* (HM Treasury *et al.* 2004), and indeed, through the whole *Every Child Matters* agenda (HM Treasury 2003), the impact of parenting is evident throughout childhood. This is particularly true of the first years, when the impact of protecting or disadvantaging factors – the first keeping children safe and engaged in society, the second frequently placing them under stress and making them more vulnerable than others to poor physical and mental health – is of prime significance. In a discussion centred on 'Understanding the particular risks relating to family and parenthood in the first two years' (though not exclusively), the following examples of disadvantaging factors are cited (Sutton and Murray 2004: 30):

- postnatal depression;
- impaired bonding;
- insecure attachment;
- low levels of cognitive stimulation and language delay;
- harsh and neglectful parenting;
- maltreatment in childhood;
- characteristics and temperament (of the child).

Defining and describing the potential impact on young children whose mothers suffer postnatal depression (together with general adversity), the authors identify research evidence showing some child behaviour problems in the children of depressed mothers which, at times is shown to lead to impaired bonding – that is, the relationship between the mother and child may be compromised, resulting in fewer interactions, with potential effects on levels of emotional, social and cognitive functioning in the young child. Attachment behaviour, first identified by Bowlby (1951, 1953, 1969), and defined as behaviour 'demonstrated by the baby towards the parent' (Sutton and Murray 2004: 30) was subsequently categorized by Ainsworth (later extended by Main and Solomon 1986) who observed children and their parent(s) in a 'strange situation', that is, one where the parent left the child in the presence of another (unfamiliar person) for short periods of time. Following their parents' return, the children's responses were then noted (Ainsworth *et al.* 1974). These observations led to recognition of several categories of behaviour which included one in which children showed they were securely attached to their parent(s), that is, they were able to separate happily, and were to keen to return for support in times of fear; and several showing children's varying uncertainty about the relationship, indicating that some felt insecure, ambivalent or resistant or, in some cases, wished to avoid their parents or caregivers completely, on their return.

Parents frequently base their behaviour as parents on their experiences of being a child. Parenting styles vary from those which provide the child with high levels of affection and acceptance to those which exert varying levels of control, ranging from indulgent to outright neglect of the child (Sutton and Murray 2004: 30). Further factors influencing parental style are thought to be the child's characteristics and their temperament, that is, whether the child is 'a bright little button' as one student revealed she had been described by her teacher, or not: a child who is, sometimes, perceived as less outgoing and less attractive or rewarding by the parent (and others). This is a particular risk for children with some impairment who may not make eye contact or who, for one reason or another, appear to be somewhat isolated. In the *Birth to Three Matters* pack (DfES 2002), we are reminded on one of the component cards that: 'Some babies who are blind or deaf or who have severe learning difficulties need constant reminders that you are there, and that they are valued'.

For children with such additional needs practice will be differentiated to include them, and the *Birth to Three Matters* framework offers a number of practical examples as to how this might be achieved. In just one component card the following points are raised:

> The need to respond warmly to a child whatever your personal feelings. Although their responses may differ, children with disabilities or learning difficulties are entitled to the same range of experiences as others. Respond positively to children who constantly seek attention or are disruptive, without reprimanding or dismissing them.
>
> (DfES 2002)

Low levels of cognitive stimulation may arise from some of the conditions discussed and, equally, neglectful parenting, in which the needs of the adult take precedence over those of the child (for whatever reason), can result in children failing to thrive and develop at an optimum rate.

Finally, maltreatment and harsh practices can often lead to children becoming hyper-vigilant in expectation of future disturbance, based on earlier frightening experiences of unpredictable events, moods, behaviours and/ or relationships in the environment. Indeed evidence indicates that 'the peak age for suffering abuse is in the first year of life' (Hosking and Walsh 2005: 17) and a major outcome of having been abused or maltreated in the early years is an increased propensity to violence. In effect, it is argued that 'Babies brought up in violent families are incubated in terror' and that because 'the early years are critically important to the child's later social development ... The result can be aggressive personalities for life' (Hosking and Walsh 2005: 17).

Undoubtedly many factors can be disturbing and have an adverse effect on a young child, and it is therefore important that action is taken, as soon as possible, to reduce the impact of these.

Protective factors preventing disadvantage for children rely, not surprisingly, on countering some of these influences and substituting others, especially through encouraging:

- strong relationships with parents, family members and other significant adults;
- parental interest and involvement in education;
- positive role models;
- active involvement in family, school and community (HM Treasury 2003:18).

The *Birth to Three Matters* framework is underpinned by recognition of the power of these influences. Alongside supporting individuals to feel recognized and valued, such factors enhance the individual's sense of self and their feelings of autonomy and self-efficacy. In view of this, it is evident why the government has been so intent on encouraging effective partnerships between parents and practitioners, since involving parents (in early years settings) appears to offer the best defence against many of the disadvantaging factors that can abound in a child's formative years.

Recent findings from a government review of literature concerning parental involvement indicated that 'In essence parenting has its influence indirectly through shaping the child's self concept as a learner and through setting high aspirations' (Desforges and Abouchaar 2003: 5). It is unsurprising therefore that 'since New Labour took office there has been a rapid escalation in the range and scale of parenting interventions', and that '40 percent of family support services' were established 'within the first five years of their return to power in 1997' (Henricson 2003: 3). Clearly, the significant role of parents in their children's lives, not only as attachment figures, but also as role models for what it is to be a social being, a member of a family group and a citizen of a democratic state is immense.

Until relatively recently, many initiatives promoted by the government focused only on parents of school-age children and these centred around 'a) providing parents with information, b) giving parents a voice and c) encouraging parental partnership with schools' (Desforges and Abouchaar 2003: 5). These have led, in turn, to the enhancement of parent governor roles, the involvement of parents in inspection, provision to them of annual reports and prospectuses, the requirement for home-school agreements and the provision of increasing amounts of information about school curriculum and performance in Standard Assessment Tests (SATs) (Desforges and Abouchaar 2003: 5). More recently this has encompassed feedback to parents of younger children, as profiles relating to the progress of children from age 3 to the end of the Reception year in schools are built up and parents are invited to contribute and share in the development of these (QCA/DfES 2002).

However, while interventions targeted at older children and their parents have been far-reaching and plentiful none has been as extensive as the Sure Start programme, launched in 1998, which to date has spent more than £3 billion on establishing approximately 520 local programmes in the most deprived areas, dedicated to 'achieve better outcomes for children, parents and communities by increasing the availability of childcare for all children; improving children's health, educational and emotional development; and supporting parents in their role and in developing employment aspirations' (www.literacytrust.org.uk;www.spiked-online.com).

Support to parents has also included, among a raft of other measures, a commitment to a goal of 12 months paid maternity leave for mothers, preceded initially by extending mothers' entitlement to paid maternity leave to 9 months from April 2007 together with the introduction of paternity leave from April 2003. This is not an unexpected bonus from a government which 'considers the promotion of good parenting as a significant tool for fostering social cohesion' (Henricson 2003: 3). At the same time, policy has encouraged parents of young children to take up employment in order to raise their own and their children's standards of living and to reduce the negative factors which sometimes lead to social exclusion, though this message has recently been tempered by a 'health warning', indicating that 'a number of studies suggest that full-time maternal employment during the very early stages of a child's life can have some small negative effects on the development of some children' (DfES 2004: 7).

Findings from research into the effects of non-parental childcare on babies' and young children's development by an internationally recognized expert in the field of child development, suggests that the bad news for parents whose children 'begin in non-maternal care in their first year or two of life for long hours, and continue at such levels until they begin school, [is that they] are somewhat more aggressive and disobedient than other children', irrespective of the quality of care they receive. However, more positively it is argued that 'when the quality of child care is good – that is, caregivers are attentive, responsive, stimulating and affectionate – children start school with enhanced cognitive-linguistic abilities, irrespective of whether they have spent time with childminders, nannies, or in centres' (www.bbc.ac.uk/news/bbkmag/17/making.html).

Further findings from longitudinal research suggest that 'young children who are looked after by their mothers do significantly better in development tests than those cared for in nurseries, by childminders or relatives' (www.guardian.co.uk). This is an issue which may cause distress to those parents who for one reason or another have elected to give the care of their children over to others. However, if what is on offer provides what Gerhardt suggests is good for babies, that is ... 'Babies need a caregiver who identifies with them so strongly that the baby's needs feel like hers ... If she feels bad when the baby feels bad, she will then want to do something about it immediately, to relieve the baby's discomfort' then substitute care could indeed effectively meet the needs of babies and young children. (Gerhardt 2004: 23).

It is important to note that, while any negative effects on children's well-being are unwelcome, what still remains unknown is the extent to which high-quality childcare can offset the disadvantaging effects of maternal or homecare for children in vulnerable families. If such research were conducted it would need to focus on many factors, including the very complex issue of the quality and consistency of one-to-one care of the child by a key person. This is particularly significant in the light of a continuing issue in childcare – that is, staff turnover, often attributed to low pay and long hours, which frequently leads to attrition when better-paid, less demanding work is offered. Another factor influencing the availability of a key person for a child, and hence the quality of care, is the adult:child ratio[1] currently set at 1:3 for babies in their first year; 1:4 for 1-2-year-olds; 1:8 for 2-3-year-olds and 1:15 for 4- and-5-year-olds.

Clearly, if staff in early years settings are to try to replicate the type of care consistent with 'good' parenting described in the literature, their practice will need to be informed by a) what parents do that is effective in enhancing outcomes for children and b) what they, themselves, would need to do in order to substitute in some ways for that care. However, the demands on caregivers in daycare settings are already complex – both in relation to the practical aspects of their work discussed above and in the requirement that they should be able to 'tune in' to a child in the loving way described by Gerhardt. The latter is complex for several reasons. First, it assumes that the individual is able accurately to identify and respond positively to their own needs so that they are able to recognize and accept the young child's feelings. Second, that they are capable of empathy – able to de-centre sufficiently to project into the often strong feelings expressed as a result of the young child's changing emotions.

Positive relationships seem to hold the key to emotional well-being, since it is known that a strong antidote to the risks children encounter in families where there is considerable stress is in having 'at least one nurturing relationship'. Evidence of this derives from a study of 698 vulnerable children, of whom it was found that approximately a third appeared 'Vulnerable but invincible' (Werner 1996), resulting from them having just one positive relationship in their lives. The same point has been argued by others: 'A good self concept largely comes from knowing those closest to you are on your side' (Manning-Morton and Thorp 2003: 14). Being 'on a child's side' is a fundamental part of the role of a key person in daycare, whose involvement with a

[1] DfES/DWP Sure Start (2003) Full Day Care: National Standards for under 8's Day Care and Child Minding, DfES publications, Nottingham.

child's parents will inevitably increase in response to difficult circumstances. While carers may not be as accurate as many parents in tuning in to babies' and children's emotional states, many succeed in making a hugely positive impact on the lives of the children they care for, so their contribution should not be underestimated.

Ultimately though, where very young children are concerned, there is no substitute for daily unconditional love from the people who have their best interests at heart: parents. As a result, a number of conclusions can be drawn about why parents matter where young children are concerned, since it is widely-held that in optimum circumstances they provide for their young:

- *emotional nurture* – through forming warm, loving bonds on which children subsequently base their assumptions about themselves (as worthy or unworthy) and other relationships;
- *social companionship* – through the acts of communication, both verbal and non-verbal, that they share with their child (Trevarthen 2001);
- *cognitive and language stimulation* – through the events of their daily life – such as visits to the park, or through 'bugging and nudging – encouraging them to display some special ability' – for example singing a nursery rhyme for a grandparent; using 'pet names', which seem to act as a binding function and being involved in 'idiosyncratic behaviour' – 'meaning [engaging in] shared rituals that the child or family members have evolved' (David *et al.* 2003: 122);
- *care to promote their physical and mental health and well-being* – through, among other things, providing regular and systematic access to medical services and preventative programmes such as injections, as well as attending child health clinics and providing sufficient food, clothing, exercise and rest to promote the child's growth and development.

The importance to the child of having a second or subsidiary positive relationship when they are in the out-of-home setting cannot be over-stated since, when children are separated from their primary important person, practitioners, their substitutes, matter almost as much.

In conclusion, it would seem that in addition to their highly significant work with children, another major role for early years settings is in continuing to offer support to parents in the things that are known to be effective. Initially these may include home visits; offering parent training programmes and fact-based advice to parents; sharing behavioural interventions that focus on helping parents develop skills; and the provision of parents-as-educators courses. However, much more collaborative and creative partnerships between parents and practitioners grow and develop when, through reflection and evaluation, practitioners question their own practice and challenge their assumptions about working with parents.

The *Birth to Three Matters* framework and *Birth to Three Matters: Review of the Literature* (David *et al.* 2003) are helpful in illustrating and identifying some of the ways in which this can be achieved. Fundamental principles expressed in *Birth to Three Matters* are:

- parents and families are central to the well-being of the child
- a relationship with a key person at home and in the setting is essential to young children's well-being (DfES 2002).

Implicit in both these statements is a commitment to the vital role parents play in their children's lives; however, many factors militate against families and without support some parents do not always manage to get parenting right. Similarly, neither do practitioners always get practice with parents right. The issue of parental involvement deserves considerable further investigation, since getting it right requires sensitivity on behalf of practitioners, commitment on behalf of settings, funding from government and a willingness from parents to partake. Sometimes it is easier to pay lip-service to a principle than to become fully immersed in what is often a life-changing process, and one which requires real commitment.

Recognizing that parents matter to their children is a huge and obvious truism yet, unless and until this truth becomes central to and embedded in practice we may merely be going through the motions of partnership. What is urgently needed now is an unequivocal recognition of the value for children of parents and carers working together with practitioners. Parents really matter to their children. Working with parents effectively will ensure that practitioners offer a safe pair of hands to both them and their children.

Reflection

The principles in the *Birth to Three Matters* framework essentially state that parents (and practitioners) matter. Early years settings may wish to consider the following points when evaluating their commitment to this approach:

- the type of support they offer new parents as they negotiate their roles;
- the extent to which they recognize and deal sensitively with parents who are 'juggling' several roles;
- how they support parents who feel 'guilty' about leaving their children in out-of-home care;
- how they free key workers to spend more time with particular chil-

dren in their group when special circumstances arise, such as if a parent is ill, hospitalized or absent for some reason from the child's life either permanently or temporarily;
- how they build non-judgemental and supportive relationships with parents whose views challenge them, or whose behaviours, attitudes and/or childrearing practices are different from their own;
- how account is taken of the diverse and dynamic nature of families where, for example, stepfamilies come together from time to time.

References

Ainsworth, M., Bell, S.M. and Stayton, D.J. (1974) Infant-mother attachment and social development: 'socialisation' as products of reciprocal responsiveness to signals, in M.P.M. Richards (ed.) *The Integration of a Child into a Social World.* Cambridge: Cambridge University Press.
Bowlby, J. (1951) *Maternal Care and Mental Health.* Report to the World Health Organization. Geneva: World Health Organization.
Bowlby, J. (1953) *Child Care and the Growth of Love.* Harmondsworth: Penguin.
Bowlby, J. (1969) *Attachment and Loss Volume 1: Attachment.* New York: Basic Books.
David, T., Goouch, K., Powell, S. and Abbott, L. (2003) *Birth to Three Matters: A Review of the Literature.* London: DfES Publications.
Desforges, C. and Abouchaar, A. (2003) *The Impact of Parental Involvement, Parental Support and Family Education on Pupil Achievement and Adjustment: A Literature Review.* London: DfES Publications.
DfES (2002) *Birth to Three Matters.* London: DfES Publications.
DfES (2004) *Five Year Strategy for Children and Learners.* London: DfES Publications.
Gerhardt, S. (2004) *Why Love Matters.* London: Routledge.
Henricson, C. (2003) *Government and Parenting: Is There a Case for a Policy Review and a Parents' Code?* York: Joseph Rowntree Foundation/YPS.
HM Treasury (2003) *Every Child Matters.* Norwich: TSO.
HM Treasury, DfES, DWP and DTI (2004) *Choice for Parents, the Best Start for Children: a Ten Year Strategy for Childcare.* London: HM Treasury.
Hosking, G and Walsh, I. (2005) *The Wave Report 2005: Violence and What to do About it.* Croydon: Wave Trust.
Main, M. and Solomon, J. (1986) Discovery of an insecure-disorganized/ disoriented attachment pattern, in T.B. Brazelton and M.W. Yogman (eds) *Affective Development in Infancy.* Nowrood, NJ: Ablex.
Manning-Morton, J. and Thorp, M. (2003) *Key Times for Play: The First Three Years.* Maidenhead: Open University Press.
NFPI (National Family and Parenting Institute) Factsheet 1 October 2003, *The Family Today: An At-a-glance Guide*, 3rd edn. London: NFPI.

Page, A. (2002) *Changing Times: Support for Parents and Families During Pregnancy and the First Twelve Months*. London: National Parenting and Family Institute.

Putnam, R.D. (2000) in M.K. Smith (2001) *Social Capital, the Encyclopaedia of Informal Education*, www.infed.org/biblio/social_capital.htm.

QCA/DfES (2002) *Foundation Stage Profile*. London: QCA.

Sutton, C. and Murray, L. (2004) Birth to two years, in C. Sutton, D. Utting and D. Farrington (eds) *Support from the Start*. Nottingham: DfES Publications.

Trevarthen, C. (2001) Intrinsic motives for companionship in understanding: their origin, development and significance for infant mental health, *Infant Mental Health Journal*, 22(1–2): 95–131.

Werner, E.E. (1996) Vulnerable but invincible: high risk children from birth to adulthood, *European Child and Adolescent Psychiatry*, 5 (suppl.1): 47–51.

World Bank (1999) *What is Social Capital?* www.worldbank.org/poverty/scapital/whatsc.html.

2 Becoming a Family

Clare Crowther

The appearance of a chapter in this book, written as I became a new mother, is explained by my work with and interest in young children, especially those between birth and 3. I was working as an early years practitioner at Bridgwater Early Excellence Centre when the publication of the *Birth to Three Matters* framework (DfES 2002) was first mooted. Having first sought the permission of my manager, I contacted Lesley Abbott and her team at Manchester Metropolitan University (MMU) and invited them to come to Bridgewater to look at our practice with children up to the age of 3. What was most distinctive about our practice, as far as we were concerned, was that our children were organized in family groups, rather than in the more traditional same-age groups, so we felt that the perspective we could offer the team was unique and worthy of their consideration. During the subsequent development of the *Birth to Three Matters* framework I and my colleagues became fully involved as it was planned and formulated, and as a result we have continued to remain involved and interested in working with MMU on issues related to work with babies and young children. So, when I became pregnant with my first child, Eve, I was delighted to be invited to write this chapter exploring the issues my husband and I faced as together we became a newly-constituted family following Eve's birth. At the same time, I felt inspired to reflect on much of what the *Birth to Three Matters* framework had to say about young children. I anticipated my child's birth with the uncertainty of every new mother and the knowledge and experience of a practitioner who had worked with children for many years. I began to record my thoughts about this process, and in my first entry after her birth I wrote: 'It has been the most exhilarating, magical and inspirational journey in my life so far, she amazes me at every turn, sharing, learning, loving and living together is beyond anything I have ever experienced before'. In this chapter, I aim to share this most intimate journey, one we have experienced together: that of becoming a family, facing the fears and challenges it has brought, along with the joys and delights of sharing in the growth of our daughter Eve.

The chapter will celebrate the achievements and recognize the process involved in becoming a family with a new baby, with particular reference to the *Birth to Three Matters* framework and its influence on a new family. I will highlight the weave of previous experience and learnt theory with the reality of everyday life as parents of a new baby. Throughout the chapter, diary entries will be used along with photographic evidence to support my account of this important journey.

Awaiting the arrival

Throughout the months we were expecting Eve there was a great deal of processing for both myself and Steve. The joy and celebrations of her safe growth and approaching arrival were shared with feelings of fear and uncertainty, many of these stemming from the knowledge that the journey we were about to undertake was the most important to face us, a journey of responsibility and challenges, knowing that the decisions we were to make would affect not only our own lives but also this new life that would be dependent upon us.

Experiences of working with families in crisis, supporting parents in their own parenting and sharing in the difficulties faced by them, together with quality professional development, left me in no uncertainty about how vast the role of being a mother was going to be. This, together with my knowledge of child development and of how, as a parent, I would hold the influences that would shape the growth, development and learning of my child made me want to do only the best for my baby, but how was this going to be possible with the demands so great? My diary entry as I anticipated Eve's birth read: 'I feel really excited, I have wanted this for a while, but feel so worried that I won't make a good parent. I've never done anything this huge before'.

That magical moment

Eve Amelia Ann was born on 29 August 2004. After a long labour, but a natural delivery, she weighed in at a healthy 8lbs 9.5ozs. To share in her birth with us was her maternal grandmother, Ann.

Eve was delivered at 10.19 a.m. and was immediately placed onto me where we shared in skin-to-skin contact, her eyes wide and looking at me for acceptance. From this moment onwards, Eve played her part in the conversations we were to hold: 'she seeks to be looked at, she works out facial patterns and expressions, she finds comfort in our faces' (DfES 2002). The language and looks we share continue to tell me her needs and wishes. What we noted is aptly described in the *Birth to Three Matters* framework: 'Young babies are sociable from birth, using a variety of ways to gain attention; being physically close and making eye contact, using touch or voice provides an ideal opportunity for early "conversations" between adults and babies' (DfES 2002).

Once Eve was born the concerns we had had throughout the term of the pregnancy disappeared, and were replaced by feelings of indescribable love

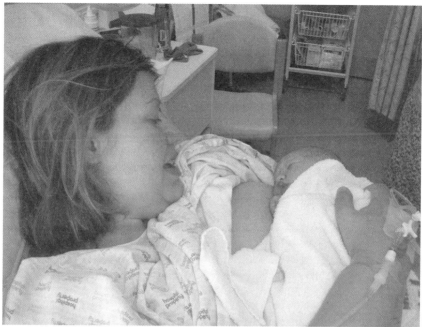

Figure 1: Clare holding Eve

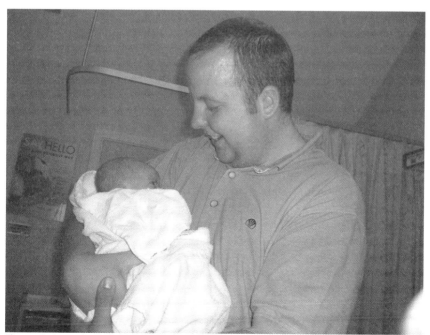

Figure 2: Steve holding Eve

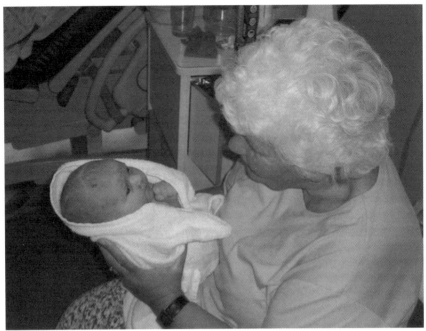

Figure 3: Mum holding Eve

and warmth, indeed these were almost overwhelming; and we were grateful for her safe arrival. She was a baby who immediately held a place within our hearts and our lives, and very quickly it became apparent that Eve was an equal member in this new partnership.

Steve my husband, Eve and I returned to our home as a family six hours after Eve's birth. Eve's maternal grandparents collected us from the maternity unit and stayed with us in our home for the first few hours while we settled in to this new feeling of family life. When they left us, we all settled together in bed, holding each other physically close, with Eve sleeping on our chests. Steve and I had a gentle awareness of her soft breath and her vulnerability – present even in sleep.

Those first few weeks

The first few weeks of becoming a family were a period of great adjustment, a time for almost immediate acceptance with little opportunity for reflection and discussion. The learning that was taking place was intense, and demanding of us all. Our new priority of a young baby, and a will to succeed at this new task called 'parenting' meant that 'after Eve' life was turned completely upside down. Fortunately, Steve was able to take the full two weeks paternity leave entitlement allowed to him, which was our saving. We were able to take every opportunity to share in this new wondrous delight of our daughter together, and also in the sleep deprivation and challenges facing us daily!

Time was taken simply to *be*. Mornings started a little later, and the realization that for the three of us to leave the house as a family, for even the shortest period, we needed one hour's preparation, two bags, a car seat and pram, together with blankets, and the all-time favourite muslin squares, [nappies] made going out together both a task and a triumph.

The special time we had in those first few weeks was so important. The relationship that Eve shares with her father is one of deep mutual love based on respect. The first few weeks of being together, and allowing Eve and our love for her to lead the way, I am sure enabled this relationship to continue to grow from strength to strength. The *Birth to Three Matters* framework states that 'Young babies are social beings; they crave close attachments with a special person … ' (DfES 2002) – and we found this to be true.

The additional support we received throughout those first few weeks was vast. Our midwife, Jenny, showed compassion and empathy and we shared a mutual respect for each other's professional knowledge. Jenny would visit our home daily and offer just the right degree of support for that particular day; she had the valuable skill of being able to 'read' us as a whole family, with a

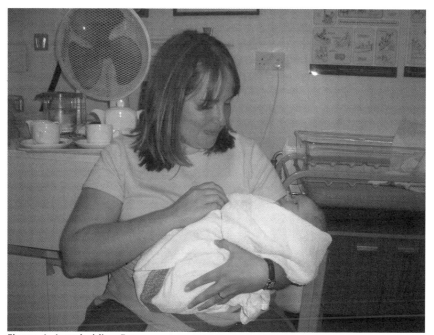

Figure 4: Aunt holding Eve

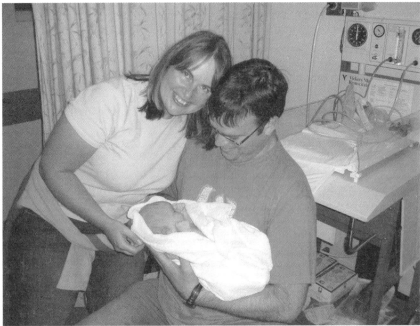

Figure 5: Aunt & Uncle with Eve

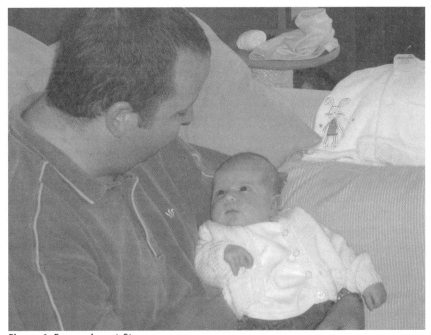

Figure 6: Eve gazing at Steve

natural intuition that gave her the ability to offer reassurance and advice without conveying any judgement or expectation. She was able to join us in our journey without intruding into our special time together, and she gave us the psychological space to feel excited, joyous and scared, all at the same time, yet offered the gentle reassurance that she was there should we need her.

The *Birth to Three Matters* framework states that 'key persons need to be able to work with any family' and, it suggests that it is important to: 'Establish shared understandings between home and setting' (DfES 2002). While this statement refers to daycare provision I feel it is equally valid for the relationship between a midwife and a parent in their own home. It was certainly significant in our case.

As both Steve and I were at home almost constantly for two weeks and I was fortunate enough not to suffer from postnatal depression, the focus of our time was very much on Eve as she gently grew. The first week was spent simply loving her, and coming to terms with this new small person sharing in our lives, our home and our time, and receiving the vast number of visitors who wanted to share with us in our pride and joy. The moments we were able to share undisturbed gave us the opportunity to really watch Eve, as already the recognition that she was changing, developing, responding and learning had begun to dawn on us. Professionally I knew that this would happen, however as a new mum the realization was mind-blowing. How could this little person be changing already? I felt I hadn't got to know her yet.

Taking the time just to be with Eve was an amazing opportunity; we were able to learn about her and to explain to her all about us. In this time, I learnt how she liked to hold my fingers as she fed, how she felt safer bathing alongside me rather than having the bath to herself, how the purring of the cats made her head turn, and her father's sneezing made her jump. It was magical to notice how she recognized my voice, and to see how the music that we had played when she was inside my womb would now settle her at night. Eve was like a sponge, she absorbed all that we offered her, showing her interest and pleasure through eye contact and a gentle gurgle that we both learnt to read as Eve's voice. The *Birth to Three Matters* framework helpfully recommends that adults 'observe and note the sounds and facial expressions young babies make in response to affectionate attention from their parents'. It also reminds us that babies and young children 'listen and respond appropriately to the language of others, including making playful and serious responses'. It argues further that, 'long before young babies can communicate verbally, they listen to, distinguish and respond to intonations in adults' voices' (DfES 2002). We were able both to read about this and then observe it happening before our very eyes!

Very quickly we wanted to extend Eve's experiences, while allowing her time to consolidate the mass of current learning she was engaged in. We surrounded her with rich textures and materials, supporting her sensual de-velopment by introducing her to the feel of voile and of sheepskin, the smell of lavender and of citrus and cinnamon in scent bags, and the sight of lava lamps, fairy lights, and black and white pictures.

We saw Eve as psychologists and others had described (Piaget and In-helder 1969; Bruce and Meggitt 1996; Bruce 1997) as an active learner; acting as a young scientist exploring her environment and experimenting with play materials, making discoveries for herself. We were aware that the *Birth to Three Matters* framework suggested that adults should 'Provide experiences that involve using all the senses, such as relaxing music, soft lighting, and pleasant smells for babies to enjoy' (DfES 2002).

Eve's learning intensified; she was deepening her awareness of her sur-roundings and loved all the opportunities offered to her. We were able to observe her, as her parents and also as professionals with knowledge of child development. We felt supported by having access to the *Birth to Three Matters* framework, using it as a guide and feeling confident as we read the support material, affirming our own findings and offering additional suggestions to enhance our skills in our new role as parents.

Eve has continued to grow and develop, spending long periods of time working and growing with me, her mother, her main carer and educator. She

Figure 7: Eve looking at Pics

has learnt to engage in problem-solving, negotiating and developing an awareness of herself and of me, and to understand the language of our bodies.

Eve has a very relaxed temperament; she was at ease with herself almost immediately and within our home she began developing new relationships, spending time with her maternal family on a daily basis. Very quickly these relationships grew in value, and 'Nana' became an important person to Eve. Eve experienced and sought closeness with her grandmother, she looked to be recognized, and found comfort in the relationship she was developing. In this way Eve was experiencing what it felt like to be acknowledged and affirmed and this continues to support her growth.

Weeks to months

The number of relationships Eve developed with other people grew over the first few weeks and months, and as motherhood and family life became more familiar to myself and Steve, we ventured further from home. Eve thrived on new relationships and always showed an underlying trust that whichever situation I asked her to participate in she would rise to the challenge and find her own way through, with love and support, trusting that she would never be far from me, and I would not allow her to be harmed.

Eve's awareness of her environments grew; she now began to recognize the farm (her maternal grandparents' home) and the large number of extended family members who would congregate there daily for employment and meals together. She experienced life in a wider family, bound together by shared values and mutual support.

The time Eve and I were sharing together was becoming more and more important to us both and when Eve was 4 months old I began to have doubts about my initial plans to shortly return to work. I knew in my heart that I was not ready to leave her in someone else's care, and that because she was my baby her need for me was still great. Perhaps my need for her was also great? So a new journey began – one about making new choices for Eve, myself and Steve.

We began by visiting a variety of care settings, and with both my professional knowledge and intuition as a mother I reluctantly concluded that none were right for us as a family. So the decision was made that I would extend my maternity leave and continue to care for Eve at home. When this choice was made another chapter of motherhood opened ahead of me: I was now to be a full-time mum, and this knowledge eased all my previous anxieties and concerns. The expectation I had of myself to be able to work and parent equally well and give both the commitment I knew they deserved was now erased, so our journey as a family started to change even further this realization was critical since it made me more aware of the fact that I had felt that there was a choice to be made, when other parents, particularly those from disadvantaged groups, may feel that they have none. Furthermore it made me more aware than ever how important it is for professionals to be able to empathize with the anxieties many parents face as they place their children in the care of others. This is often easier said than done, since without experiencing the crushing love I experienced for Eve, I do not think I could have ever truly understood what parents really go through as they leave their children in our care.

Sharing in Eve's learning

The opportunity to spend the next eight months at home with Eve excited me, however it also brought with it its own set of dilemmas. I had always been passionate about my career and knew I was going to miss the additional dimensions that work offered to my life; I therefore made the decision to continue my involvement in the Birth to Three Matters project with MMU. This, together with caring for Eve, worked incredibly well for us all, and it took no time at all before I realized what a fortunate position I was in. Here I was sharing in the growth and learning of my own daughter while contributing to training others in ways of working with babies and young children. 'What better place to be?' I asked myself.

As I began to study Eve more purposefully, the observation and identification of each stage of her learning was now documented closely and shared with the groups I was working with. This helped me to be slightly more detached in the recognition of her needs and in terms of learning. My baby now had the equivalent of a possible line of direction chart (PLOD), as used by the Pen Green Centre to support the identification and possible extension of ideas for her current and future learning and development.

The dialogue and documentation that I had undertaken professionally with parents I was working alongside concerning their own children's learning had always been of great interest to me. I valued the opportunity to share in others' understanding of the individual child, and to reflect upon the experiences and environment provided to ensure it was meeting the best interests of the child. Discussing theory and our observation with parents, identifying, observing, planning and reflecting equally in partnership with them now allowed me to discuss Eve's progress and development as a point of shared information. She became both the focus for my love as a parent and of my work as a practitioner, offering me ready examples of a young child's growth, play and learning.

Using the *Birth to Three Matters* framework to support our understanding of Eve has enabled me to identify how she is developing in each of the aspects of the framework, as a Strong Child, a Skilful Communicator, a Competent

Learner and a Healthy Child. As she began her own amazing journey through the broad development area, described in the *Birth to Three Matters* framework as a 'Heads up, Looker and Communicator' we identified Eve as a Strong Child. Eve found comfort in touch and in the human face; she enjoyed the company of others and felt safe and loved. She loved to snuggle in, looking for acceptance and recognition from others.

Eve was also developing as a Competent Learner. She was exploring and discovering all the time, and she would make playful interactions, mimicking the adults and children in her social circle. She was using sensory exploration to connect with her environment, using her senses to discover and investigate, making connections and beginning to understand the world around her.

As a Skilful Communicator Eve was developing well, since from birth she had been able to convey messages about her needs and wants. This was now increasing to preferences, and extended to communicating how she was feeling. Eve was communicating her meaning, ensuring that she was being understood, as she learnt her voice had an effect on others' actions. She was, and continues to be, very sociable and has developed strong social relationships. She has shown that she is able to listen and respond, finding her own voice, and is developing into a competent and confident language user.

Eve was also developing as a Healthy Child. She knew that she was, and continues to be, very special to many people. She is able to discover her own boundaries and limits. She is encouraged to take risks and use her physical skills, discovering for herself about her own body and what she can do and what she enjoys.

Moving on

Eve has continued to grow and learn as we have offered her new experiences and the freedom to investigate and explore at her own pace, revisiting her previous learning and through having her wishes responded to positively. She is strong minded, with a developing sense of her own well-being and self-worth. Described by her grandmother as 'feisty and wilful', she creates her own agendas and carries them through with determination and high levels of concentration. This is accurately described in the *Birth to Three Matters* framework as 'warm, mutual affirmative relationships give babies the courage to express their feelings'. I am sure the value being placed on Eve as an individual will have enhanced her determination and will to participate with others. She has consistently shown deep levels of involvement in her play, and through close observation and use of the support materials from the *Birth to Three Matters* framework we have been able to offer her appropriate activities to enhance her learning and development.

Many other changes have taken place for us as a family throughout this time. The choice was made to home-share with my parents, creating opportunities for Eve to develop closer relationships with her maternal grandparents and her aunts, uncles and cousins, who have become strong daily influences. The care and parenting of Eve has therefore grown wider. There are now six adults responding daily to Eve and her needs and wishes. She is able to explore her relationship with each of these significant adults in her life and has quickly learnt who responds to different aspects of her behaviour and personality; she knows who she likes to snuggle with, who she likes to laugh with and who is best to share a slice of toast with! This exemplifies the *Birth to Three Matters* framework statement recognizing that 'babies develop an understanding and awareness of themselves, which is influenced by their family, culture, other people and the environment' and another which reminds us that 'to sustain healthy emotional attachments babies need familiar, trusting safe and secure relationships'.

The ease with which Eve has fitted into this deeply complex structure of extended family life has amazed us all. She may well be the youngest of the family but she still has the ability to have her voice not just heard but really listened to, and has developed a strong sense of self from being recognized as an important member of the whole family. This high level of well-being has given her the confidence to build new relationships outside her family circle.

As parents we recognize how much we have shown Eve our love, and how much she feels supported and nurtured by the presence of her family. However we have also recognized the need for Eve to begin to extend these relationships to children of her own age and decided that Eve would attend the children's centre where I worked, to begin to build friendships with other children, learning the new skills of cooperation and negotiation which she was starting to find challenging at home, surrounded only by adults.

At present Eve is continuing with her settling-in visits, building a new relationship with her key person at the centre and the 'key family' members she will join there, loving the opportunities on offer and confirming for us that the choice we made for me to stay at home with her for the first year of her life was the right one. As a family it has meant forgoing certain elements of our previous lifestyle; we have given up our own home and our privacy as a nuclear family temporarily, but the rewards of watching an already happy baby grow into an even more confident, independent, sociable, aware and capable baby have been worth every difficulty we have been faced with.

As a family we have continued to grow; as individuals, as partners and as parents. At each stage we have taken time to discuss, reflect on and share our new responsibilities. Communication between us has grown and we have welcomed the opportunity to plan together, ensuring that we are providing the best possible experiences we can for Eve. As we look back over the last year we realize that no training, no past experiences and no one piece of advice could have prepared us for the journey we have undertaken. Now, standing at the crossroads of expecting our second baby, as I draw this chapter to a close, the dawning realization that becoming a family containing two children under 14 months old, will start a whole new chapter in our family life is both thrilling and daunting – we have learnt a great deal and we have much left still to learn. We know that we have done what most parents try to do as their family increases its membership; we hope that we can be 'good-enough' parents (Winnicott 1971: 13). We know that many families are not as blessed as we are. We know that our future work as professionals will be influenced by learning from our experience of parenthood, by recognizing that every family is different and by acknowledging that there are many ways to be 'good enough'. We have simply tried to do it our way.

References

Bruce, T. (1997) *Early Childhood Education*. London: Hodder & Stoughton.

Bruce, T. and Meggitt, C. (1996) *Child Care and Education*. London: Hodder & Stoughton.

DfES (2002) *Birth to Three Matters*. London: DfES Publications.

Piaget, J. and Inhelder, B. (1969) *The Psychology of the Child*. London Routledge & Kegan Paul.

Winnicott, D.W. (1971) *Playing and Reality*. London: Routledge.

3 Grandparents Matter

Tricia David

It is said that when Beethoven died, a portrait of his much-loved grandfather hung on the wall of his room. What was surprising was the fact that this grandfather had died when Beethoven was only 3 years old. However, it is thought that the man had been a loving and formative influence whom the great composer never forgot. Research on resilience (Werner 1996) indicates that having just one person to whom you matter and to whom what you do matters is crucial to your ability to cope in the face of life's stresses and strains. Sometimes the one person who gives a child that feeling of 'mattering' to someone they love is a grandparent. Clearly, the happiest scenario is for each child to matter to parents, grandparents, siblings and other family and community members.

Using the framework from *Birth to Three Matters* (DfES 2002) as the structure for this chapter about grandparenting, I will discuss the delights and possible tensions inherent in grandparenthood; research 'messages' from young children about their relationships with their grandparents; and the issues which can arise through family separation and divorce. The limited research evidence which is available about young children and their grandparents will be drawn upon, together with possible reasons why, until recently, grandparents were rarely included as important participants in the search for understanding about families and young children.

A Strong Child

Grandparents can have a powerful role in supporting a child's development, as outlined by the four components of the *Birth to Three Matters* framework concerning a Strong Child. Grandparents' knowledge of their family's history (both those who constitute the current family and those who are no longer living) means they can tell stories that help the child gain a realization of their individuality, personal characteristics and separateness from others, while at the same time helping them feel they belong and to begin to have a sense of continuity. Older children can gain an understanding of how their lives are influenced by time and place.

Some family theorists (e.g. Bengston 2001) suggest that development takes place in a historical period, so there is a period effect on how humans develop; there is a cohort effect (you and your peers form a cohort who may be affected by particular events within that historical period); and there is a lineage effect (the result of being in a particular generation of a family). For example, it is rare for young Chinese adults to have any siblings but for their children, born more recently, it is also rare for them to have any cousins, as a result of the strictness of the one-child policy over the last three decades. It is hardly surprising therefore that both these grown-up children and any children they have will be adored and prized by the older generations, particularly in a country where Confucian 'ancestor worship', respect and responsibilities towards parents and grandparents prevails. This is a stark example of the impact of period, cohort and lineage effects. These effects will impinge on an individual's understanding of who they are and how they fit in. Grandparents can directly and indirectly influence a young child's self-assurance and sense of belonging and this influence can be positive or negative.

Attachment theory (David *et al.* 2003) can help us understand the ways in which grandparents and other significant adults are models whose behaviour becomes internalized by a child. Research (Caspi and Elder 1988; Van Ijzendoorn 1995; Warner *et al.* 1999) shows how depressive illnesses, antisocial behaviour or drug taking, for example, impact on children and grandchildren. However, Plomin and Bergeman (1991) and Smith and Drew (2004) argue that some of these effects may be due to genetic factors. The current body of research into grandparenting as a whole is not extensive. Thus it is important to note that, although the evidence for intergenerational transmission seems compelling, there is only a small number of studies which indicate a consistency of attachment styles across the generations – grandmother-daughter-child. For example, Benoit and Parker (1994) explored sensitivity to infant signals. A grandparent may be having a direct influence through warm, sensitive responses to a baby or young child, but it is also likely that they have infused their relationship with their own 'child' (now the mother or father) with this sensitivity, so having an indirect effect. A similar effect has been found in relation to grandfathers whose daughters are single parents (Oyserman *et al.* 1994).

In fact, Siegel (1999) claims that parents' narratives of their own attachments to *their* parents are the best indicators of the likely warmth and responsiveness of their attachments to their own newborns. He argues that this should be explored during pregnancy and that those whose narratives indicate difficult early attachments between parent and grandparent should be helped to overcome these problems in order to ensure positive attachments for their babies.

Clearly, while indirect effects will pertain wherever grandparents live, direct effects will be leavened by the geographical distance between generations. In fact, physical proximity has been shown to be the most important factor influencing frequency of interaction and the extent of emotional closeness (Hurme 1988; Sticker 1991; Fearnley-Whittingstall 2005). But all is not lost for grandparents who live at a great distance, because, as we shall see in the next section, warm contacts that are important to the child as they become older can still be achieved. Further, research (Smith and Drew 2004) shows that grandparents feel equally emotionally attached to their grandchildren whether they are those who live too far away to visit often or those they see at least weekly. (I can endorse this from personal experience but I do worry that my 'child' and my grandchildren who live over 300 miles away may feel I cannot give them the support they need!)

At the same time, it must be said that sometimes grandparents can be seen as interfering, or as having old-fashioned ideas about childrearing which upset parents and are the cause of emotional difficulties that can have an indirect effect on the child. This is particularly poignant when older generations of a family have roots in a culture which holds different views and traditions with respect to childrearing.

A study of Muslim families in Britain (Sonuga-Barke *et al.* 1998) found that mothers who had disagreements with grandparents about their children's upbringing had high levels of anxiety and depression, because the older generation tended to be authoritarian, the mothers more child-centred. Another study of children with a Greek father and an English mother, living in Greece, found the children had difficulty embracing their grandparents' expectations concerning cultural identity (Anderson 1999).

We know from research (Konner 1991; Werner 1996) that resilient children are likely to have had at least one strong, meaningful attachment relationship which began early in their lives, although subsequent influences can reverse ill-effects (Rutter 1989; Schaffer 1998). This is likely to mean that grandparents as well as parents and other carers who have been sensitive to a child's individual needs, likes and dislikes, rituals and so on, contribute to the development of resilience.

For babies and very small children, rituals are particularly important because they help with the development of a sense of security and of having some power over what happens in their lives. One of my grandchildren who loved coming to stay at our house overnight even when she was very tiny had (and still has) various rituals associated with preparing for bedtime. Among these, when only a year old, was bouncing on our big bed, while holding hands with one of us, to repeated renditions of 'There was an old woman tossed up in a basket', complete with funny voices. On one occasion when another song was introduced she flung herself down on the bed crying, 'No, old woman, old woman!' So all other songs were excluded at this time of day.

In terms of helping a child become strong and resilient, one of the most important roles a grandparent can assume is that of emotional 'buffer' or confidante in whom older grandchildren can confide (Smith and Drew 2004). The seeds of this kind of trust are usually sown in early childhood.

A Skilful Communicator

The first time I met my twin grandsons Oliver and Sam, they were still in the hospital's premature baby unit. As my daughter and I walked to the ward I asked her if she talked to her tiny boys, because I had noticed the reticence of young parents to talk to their babies in public. My older daughter had told me, sadly, of people giving one 'funny looks'. As I leaned over the first cot and began to talk to my new grandson, he smiled the kind of smile I had been told when a young mum was 'just wind'. People tell us that my daughter and I sound the same – I think her baby recognized the 'tune' and tone of family. Excitedly I told my daughter he had smiled. I noticed the nurse who happened to be in the room smile to herself – was this because she agreed, or did she think I was deluding myself, it was 'just wind'? Researchers (Karmiloff and Karmiloff-Smith 2001) report that babies in the womb are eavesdropping on all around them, really listening to the familiar sounds, and that they can distinguish the speech patterns of their family's languages from those who speak an unfamiliar language.

This is another strand in the evidence showing how babies come into the world 'programmed' to be social creatures, to want to communicate. As grandparents we can support parents to feel confident enough not to care about the 'funny looks' and to talk to their babies wherever they are.

The drive to be near the people with whom one is most familiar (parents, siblings, grandparents) and to watch them, their facial expressions in particular, for information about the safety or otherwise of a situation (called 'social referencing') is especially strong in the first three years (Singer 2001). Further, according to Singer, tuned-in family members and carers will 'read' and respond appropriately to a child's facial expressions. However, since babies and small children are very good at 'reading' body language, they are confused when body language and spoken language do not match.

Young children's powers of observation and intent listening mean that from a surprisingly early age they know what makes those closest to them 'tick'. Dunn (1988) and Stern (1985) have shown how babies can become jokers from around 9 months of age and from 15 months will use play and language which includes teasing. 'Mind reading' (Dunn 1999) – recognizing that other people have different likes and dislikes – seems to begin during the second year and is part of the process of becoming an individual, as well as being used to create a reaction. One young child went to his grandmother while his parents worked, but there was disagreement about the use of certain language. The grandmother was criticized by the parents because she used 'baby' language such as 'doggy' and 'pussy cat' and the grandmother disapproved of the parents' propensity for swearing. On one occasion, while with the grandmother, the prize rocking horse she had bought him surged forward and hit the child on the head but did not really injure him. His grandmother was horrified to hear him yell 'F***ing geegee!', apparently prioritizing words destined to inflict maximum shock on all his significant adults.

Once children begin to talk, grandparents who know a child's first words can provide supportive encouragement. Grandparents in ethnic minority communities can often be seen as providing the strongest reason for families maintaining minority languages. However, research (Luo and Wiseman 2000) among Chinese families in the USA demonstrated that it is in fact peer interactions with other children for whom Chinese or English is the first language that has greater influence. Further, in New Zealand, Chinese grandchildren were found to have some difficulties in communicating with grandparents owing to complicated mismatches in expression (Anping *et al.* 2004). However, grandparents could be particularly helpful if enlisted by Early Childhood Education and Care (ECEC) settings to help staff maintain children's bilingualism. For as Thompson's (1999) research in the North East of England showed, by the end of their first term in nursery, children who spoke Mirpuri-Panjabi at home were using only English.

Nevertheless, all grandparents who live at a distance from their children's children and who worry that this will reduce their emotional closeness can take heart from research which shows that telephone conversations, letters and emails are effective in sustaining relationships (Age Concern 1998; Silverstein and Marenco 2001; Smith and Drew 2004). Many children under 3 will be adept telephone users, although the cost of calls can be prohibitive. Letters can be pictures, photographs and cards to start with, plus the occasional mailed gift or pocket money. Most of the grandparents who participated in Drew's (cited in Smith and Drew 2004) UK study about being separated geographically from their grandchildren spoke to them at least once every week.

A Competent Learner

Being a competent learner means one can make connections, be imaginative and creative, and represent one's ideas and understandings through the 'hundred languages of children' (Edwards *et al.* 1998). Using creativity and imagination means one can move further than representations, making transformations of knowledge, presenting new thoughts and ideas in some way. Grandparents have been shown to offer opportunities by taking children out on trips and excursions, playing games, engaging in traditional activities, such as going to parks (Powell and Goouch 2005) and telling family history stories. On excursions involving a certain amount of car travel, when any journey longer than ten minutes can seem a lifetime to a young child, we often play 'What am I?' with our grandchildren, simplifying it for 2-year-olds. For several years one grandson, now aged 7, has enjoyed choosing very obscure transformations that are often mixtures of the categories we generally use – real/imaginary, living/non-living, and so on. He can always explain how he has arrived at his 'creature' and its characteristics and we have at last become more adept at divining his line of thinking.

The ability to reflect on and piece together ideas about one's own learning – metacognition – has been shown to be connected with emotional attachment. Securely attached children are said to show greater ability in metacognition (Parkes *et al.* 1996). It is suggested that mothers of securely attached children are more likely to have treated their babies as individuals with minds, who can understand what is going on and what is being explained to them. As a result, by the age of 4 or 5 they are said to have the ability to reflect not only on their own thinking but also on that of others.

Clearly, grandparents, like parents, will only register as having positive effects on their grandchildren if they behave in ways that are valued in their communities. As Rosenthal (2003) has stated, some communities value children as the future members of their society and think they should defer to older members, learning from them, especially about rules of conduct. These societies value the community above an individual. Meanwhile, at the other extreme, is the individualistic society which places young children as the equals of adults and values their ideas and contributions. So when studies focus on what come to be seen as the quality of interactions between members of a group, the measures used and ideas of quality will depend on the kind of society envisaged. A caveat about studies of grandparenting should also therefore be stated: societies or communities with different values and traditions from the one being studied in the research may find the results do not match with their own experiences.

Similarly, contradictory evidence needs to be explored for contextual and other factors. An example of this comes from China. Falbo (1991) found that where grandparents provided preschool care the children gained better results in primary school. However, in Shanghai in 2003, our UK team was told by ECEC officials that grandparents did not provide appropriate care because they did not know about modern childrearing. The speed of change in China as a whole, and in cities like Shanghai in particular, may mean that in only a decade the expectations of young children and of those who provide care for them may be very different.

Meanwhile, research carried out in the USA (Bernal and Keane 2005) suggests that informal care by relatives is less effective than group ECEC and new research in the UK is said to show that grandparents are the least effective choice for children under 3. *The Sunday Times* (Leppard and Sanderson 2005) reports that Penny Leach has studied the lives of 1200 children for the last six years. Leach reported her findings in 2005 and discussed how the young children looked after by their mothers did significantly better on developmental tests than those who went to nurseries, childminders or informal care with relatives. As far back as the 1930s and 1940s articles criticized grandparental influences as old-fashioned and didactic (Vollmer 1937) but as yet there are no details from these research studies to indicate exactly what aspects of grandparenting relate to the children's relatively poor development. In the USA between 1980 and 1997, 1.3 million grandparents were raising their grandchildren, often because of parental divorce or incarceration, drug use, illnesses such as AIDS and child abuse. A US study found children raised by grandparents to have significantly poorer academic results at school than children raised in similar homes with their parents (Kennedy and Keeney 1988). This is thought to be the result of poverty and poor healthcare. Further, some of the grandparents had a high incidence of isolation, depression and other health problems.

Parents of children with special educational needs (SEN) are highly dependent on the emotional support of their own parents, more so than on their instrumental, practical, support (Herbert 1994; Trute 2003). While many grandparents feel deeply for both their child and their grandchild, and may themselves be disappointed and grieving over the birth of a child with a disability, others overcome this and attend groups which help them respond to their grandchild's needs. Grandparents who seek education about their grandchild's disability are said to be more accepting and involved with the grandchild (Schilmoeller and Baranowski 1999). Courses in signing for grandparents of deaf children are said to help them to interact but also to come to terms with the situation. One loving grandmother I know learnt to sign and became involved in activities at her grandson's school for the deaf, as well as further developing her ability to enjoy communicating on a one-to-one basis. Other courses for grandparents may become more widespread but may also prove controversial.

A Healthy Child

One of the important practical roles of a grandparent in relation to health is in alerting younger family members to any potentially inherited medical conditions that may need to be checked. Health professionals now know much more about the risks of inheriting heart complaints and other illnesses that can be ameliorated with lifestyle changes and/or medication.

Children's responses to parental separation and divorce can be influenced by grandparents' as well as by parents' behaviour. Drew and Smith (1999, 2002) found that grandparents can act as a 'stress buffer', providing emotional support to the children involved. Naturally, the relationship between the grandparents and the custodial parent will be crucial. There are between

200,000 and 400,000 non-custodial fathers in the UK who have lost contact with their children. Thus, there must be a huge number of grandparents who suffer pain at their sons' sadness and at being excluded from their grandchildren's lives. Judy Dunn (Nicholson 2005) is reported as adding that this suffering must be a disaster from the children's perspective too. The Grandparents' Action Group UK (www.grandparents-association.org.uk) is calling for one day a week contact to be established. Similarly, grandparents can lose contact when a child is put up for adoption and the effect can be devastating for them – there does not appear to be as yet any research detailing the effects on children.

It is not unusual now for grandparents themselves to be divorced or separated. This can mean children are blessed with more than four grandparents, since stepgrandparents can enter a child's life through a grandparent remarrying, a parent remarrying or the parent of a step-parent remarrying. Generally the length of the relationship seems to be the main factor in determining the strength of the relationship between a child and a stepgrandparent (Smith and Drew 2004), but again there have been few research studies on this topic.

Nor is there as yet very much research about gay parenting and the role of grandparents. That which has been carried out (Patterson *et al.* 1998; Gartrell *et al.* 1999) demonstrates the positive effects of grandparent contact on the well-being of children and improved relations between parents and grandparents on the arrival of the baby.

When grandparents have had close emotional bonds with grandchildren, the death of the grandparent can come as a shock but there are also children who cope and grief counsellors suggest the best person to tell the child is the parent, even if the parent is themselves weeping at the loss. This is because it is important for children to see how adults grieve and miss loved ones. Although one may wish to limit the extent to which young children are exposed to the terrible events that occur in our world, shielding children from family sadness may prevent them from developing the confidence to cope with stress.

While the death of grandparents is something families may, in a sense, be prepared for, the death of a child or grandchild is a terrible tragedy few of us expect to experience in contemporary 'northern' societies (Uhlenberg 1980). Again, there is little research on this subject but grandparents have been reported by White (1999) as carrying a triple burden – grief for their 'child' (the parent), for themselves and for the dead child or any siblings, but also showing the level of support they can give at such a time. Meanwhile, Helen Penn (2005a, 2005b) reminds us that we need to think how we can be part of the action to stop death and deprivation being a major part of the unequal childhoods of children in the Majority World. According to UNICEF, during the last decade 5 million children have died of HIV/AIDS; a further 15 million have been orphaned by the same illness; 2 million have been slaughtered and 12 million left homeless by war and conflict. Those of us in the 'north' who are fortunate to be grandparents of healthy, happy children might ask ourselves what we can do to help create a fairer world. Recognizing the effects of living in a consumer society on our grandchildren and on children in the Majority World might be one place to start.

A component of the Healthy Child (DfES 2002) is Healthy Choices but the extent to which children are allowed to make choices about their own lives is still limited. Büchner (2003) discusses families' strategies for directing children's life courses but also points to increasing agency among the young and to elements of negotiation between generations. He argues that there are more opportunities for participation for successive generations but that it is still parents and grandparents who hold the reins of power. They continue to transmit social and cultural capital to their descendants, though this could be changing with the development of the information society.

Being a grandparent

Research about grandparents is not prolific and this may have been because of the focus on the nuclear family during the middle of the twentieth century. More recently recognition of the ecology of human development (Bronfenbrenner 1979) has drawn attention to wider social reality and life span research (Rutter and Rutter 1993) has shown the influence of intergenerational interaction. In addition, there is greater acceptance of the idea that 'the family is neither a pan-human universal nor a stable or essential entity ... Families and family relations are, like the term itself, flexible, fluid and contingent' (Jagger and Wright 1999: 3). At this time, perhaps we should take a social constructionist approach and explore models of grandparenthood in the same way as models of childhood, trying to understand how and why they differ and change. Being a grandparent is an important phase in the life cycle for around 75 per cent of us, most commonly starting in our early fifties. With current mortality rates, this means we are likely to spend 25 years being grandparents and possibly even great-grandparents, although this may now decrease as many young adults are deciding not to become parents until well into their thirties. Such delays may worry potential grandparents who think their fitness levels will fall with increasing age but it may comfort those who want to use their early retirement for the adventures they believe they missed out on in youth.

The evolving role of the grandparent is full of opportunities, although some suggest it is becoming institutionalised (Hill 2002). For grandchildren, grandparents offer a richness of experience and a fund of knowledge that will no doubt be different from what their parents offer, because of their different interests and perspectives. Similarly, grandchildren keep older generations in touch with current trends. As Fearnley-Whittingstall (Millard 2005: 10) has said, despite our difficulties with modern buggies and other equipment, 'The sheer joy of being a grandmother . . . well, one is quite unprepared for it. You have no idea how much it grabs your heart'.

On a personal note, I was 'granny reared' from the age of 3 months, because my mother worked and my father was away, a soldier in World War II, throughout my first three years of life. I look back on that time and what I remember of it with great affection and admiration for all the adults and older cousins who peopled my world. It makes me want to explore research findings more deeply and helps me see the complexity of human existence. Having seven grandchildren, I know the passion and respect they inspire, for they remind one of the wonder and beauty around us and one aches for a world in which neither they nor their contemporaries will be harmed.

Research can inform policy and practice but it needs to be viewed contextually and politically. It is our real-life encounters with young children, parents and grandparents that help us reflect on research, policy and practice.

References

Age Concern (1998) *Across the Generations*. London: Age Concern.

Anderson, M. (1999) Children in-between: constructing bicultural families, *Royal Anthropological Institute*, 5: 13–26.

Anping, H., Loong, C. and Ng, S.H. (2004) Tri-generational family conversations: communication, accommodation and brokering, *British Journal of Social Psychology*, 43(3): 449–64.

Bengston, V.L. (2001) Beyond the nuclear family, *Journal of Marriage and the Family*, 63: 1–16.

Benoit, D. and Parker, K. (1994) Stability and transmission of attachment across three generations, *Child Development*, 65: 1444–56.

Bernal, R. and Keane, M.P. (2005) Maternal time, child care and child cognitive development: the case of single mothers. Paper presented at the World Congress of the Econometric Society, University College London, September.

Bronfenbrenner, U. (1979) *The Ecology of Human Development*. Cambridge, MA: Harvard University Press.

Bÿchner, P. (2003) The transmission of social and cultural capital between family generations, in B. Mayall and H. Zeiher (eds) *Childhood in Generational Perspective*. London: University of London Institute of Education.

Caspi, A. and Elder, G.H. (1988) Emergent family patterns, in R.A. Hinde and J. Stevenson-Hinde (eds) *Relationships Within Families: Mutual Influences*. Oxford: Oxford University Press.

David, T., Goouch, K., Powell, S. and Abbott, L. (2003) *Birth to Three Matters: a Review of the Literature*. London: DfES Publications.

DfES (2002) *Birth to Three Matters*. London: DfES Publications.

Drew, L. and Smith, P.K. (2002) Implications for grandparents when they lose contact with their grandchildren: divorce, family feud and geographical separation, *Journal of Mental Health and Ageing*, 8: 95–119.

Dunn, J. (1988) *The Beginnings of Social Understanding*. Cambridge, MA: Harvard University Press.

Dunn, J. (1999) Mindreading and social relationships, in M. Bennett (ed.) *Developmental Psychology*. London: Taylor and Francis.

Edwards, C., Gandini, L. and Foreman, G. (1998) *The Hundred Languages of Children*. New York: Ablex.

Falbo, T. (1991) The impact of grandparents on children's outcomes in China, *Marriage and Family Review*, 16: 369–76.

Fearnley-Whittingstall, J. (2005) *The Good Granny Guide*. London: Short Books.

Gartrell, N., Hamilton, J., Banks, A., Mosbacher, D., Reed, N., Sparks, C.H., Bishop, H. and Rodas, C. (1999) The National Lesbian Family Study: 2 interviews with mothers of toddlers, *American Journal of Orthopsychiatry*, 69: 362–9.

Herbert, E. (1994) Becoming a special family, in T. David (ed.) *Working Together for Young Children*. London: Routledge.

Hill, T.J. (2002) Grandparents in law: investigating the institutionalisation of extended family roles, *International Journal of Aging and Human Development*, 54(1): 43–56.

Hurme, H. (1988) *Child, Mother and Grandmother: Intergenerational Interaction in Finnish Families*. Jyvaskyla: University of Jyvaskyla Press.

Jagger, G. and Wright, C. (eds) (1999) *Changing Family Values*. London: Routledge.

Karmiloff, K. and Karmiloff-Smith, A. (2001) *Pathways to Language*. Cambridge, MA: Harvard University Press.

Kennedy, J.F. and Keeney, V.T. (1988) The extended family revisited: grandparents rearing grandchildren, *Child Psychiatry and Human Development*, 19: 26–35.

Konner, M. (1991) *Childhood*. London: Ebury Press.

Leppard, D. and Sanderson, D. (2005) Mother care gives children the best start, *The Sunday Times*, 2 October.

Luo, S-H. and Wiseman, R.L. (2000) Ethnic language maintenance among Chinese immigrant children in the United States, *International Journal of Intercultural Relations*, 24(3): 307–24.

Millard, R. (2005) Thoroughly modern grannies, *The Sunday Times T2*, 1 May.

Nicholson, J. (2005) 'Our rights are being ignored': on the grief of estranged grandparents, *The Times T2*, 28 February.

Oyserman, D., Radin, N. and Saltz, E. (1994) Predictions of nurturant parenting in teen mothers living in three generational families, *Child Psychiatry and Human Development*, 24(4): 215–30.

Parkes, C.M., Stevenson-Hinde, J. and Marris, P. (eds) (1996) *Attachment Across the Life Cycle*. London: Routledge.
Patterson, C.J., Hurt, S. and Mason, C.D. (1998) Families of the lesbian baby boom: children's contact with grandparents and other adults, *American Journal of Orthopsychiatry*, 68: 390–9.
Penn, H. (2005a) Do we care? *Nursery World*, 105(3988): 10–11.
Penn, H. (2005b) *Unequal Childhoods: Young Children's Lives in Poor Countries*. London: Routledge.
Plomin, R. and Bergeman, C.S. (1991) The nature of nurture, *Behaviour and Brain Sciences*, 14: 373–427.
Powell, S. and Goouch, K. (2005) Critical reflections on a project exploring young children's vies of play. Paper presented at the BERA Annual Conference, University of Glamorgan, September.
Rosenthal, M. (2003) Quality in early childhood education and care: a cultural context, *European Early Childhood Research Journal*, 11(2): 101–16.
Rutter, M. (1989) Pathways from childhood to adult life, *Journal of Child Psychology and Psychiatry*, 30: 23–51.
Rutter, M.J. and Rutter, M. (1993) *Developing Minds: Challenge and Continuity Across the Lifespan*. Harmondsworth: Penguin.
Schaffer, H.R. (1998) *Making Decisions about Children*. Oxford: Blackwell.
Schilmoeller, G.L. and Baranowski, M.D. (1999) Intergenerational support in families with disabilities: grandparents' perspectives, *Families in Society: the Journal of Contemporary Human Services*, 79: 465–76.
Siegel, D. (1999) *The Developing Mind*. New York: Guilford.
Silverstein, M. and Marenco, A. (2001) How Americans enact the grandparenting role across the family life course, *Journal of Family Issues*, 22: 493–522.
Singer, E. (2001) The logic of young children's non-verbal behaviour. Keynote address, European Early Childhood Educational Research Association Conference, Alkmaar, Netherlands, 29 August–1 September.
Smith, P.K. and Drew, L.M. (2004) Grandparenting and extended support networks, in M. Hoghughi and N. Long (eds) *Handbook of Parenting*. London: Sage.
Sonuga-Barke, E.J.S., Mistry, M. and Qureshi, S. (1998) The mental health of Muslim mothers in extended families living in Britain: the impact of intergenerational disagreement on anxiety and depression, *British Journal of Clinical Psychology*, 37: 399–408.
Stern, D.N. (1985) *The Interpersonal World of the Infant*. New York: Basic Books.
Sticker, E.J. (1991) The importance of grandparenthood during the life cycle in Germany, in P.K. Smith (ed.) *The Psychology of Grandparenthood: An International Perspective*. London: Routledge.
Thompson, L. (1999) *Young Bilingual Learners at Nursery*. Clevedon, OH: Multilingual Matters.
Trute, B. (2003) Grandparents of children with developmental disabilities: intergenerational support and family well-being, *Families and Society*, 84(1): 119–26.

Uhlenberg, P. (1980) Death and the family, *Journal of Family History*, 5: 313–20.

Van Ijzendoorn, M.H. (1995) Adult attachment representations, *Psychological Bulletin*, 117: 387–403.

Vollmer, H. (1937) The grandmother: a problem in child rearing, *American Journal of Orthopsychiatry*, 7: 378–82.

Warner, V., Weissman, M., Mufson, L. and Wickramaratne, P.J. (1999) Grandparents, parents and grandchildren at high risk for depression: a three-generational study, *Journal of American Academy of Child Adolescent Psychiatry*, 38: 289–96.

Werner, E.E. (1996) Vulnerable but invincible: high risk children from birth to adulthood, *European Child and Adolescent Psychiatry*, 5 (supp.1): 47–51.

White, D.L. (1999) Grandparent participation in times of family bereavement, in B. de Vries (ed.) *End of Life Issues*. New York: Springer Publishing.

4 Everyday Activities at Home: Meeting our Developmental Needs with our Young Children

Margaret Henry

Whilst the aim of the *Birth to Three Matters* (DfES 2002) framework is to support the development of young children it could be argued that much of what it contains has much wider applicability, encompassing a broader model – not only focusing on the well-being of children but also of their parents and carers. This chapter considers this broader model because, as the title indicates, it is about parents, practitioners and other adults as well as children. Not only does it describe how parents contribute to young children's well-being as together they take part in everyday activities at home, it also considers how their own well-being, as parents, is affected. Hence, it is argued, a framework which applies to adults as well as children is important in meeting a wide range of development needs. Such a framework would address our developmental needs as human beings, into which feed all of the aspects of the *Birth to Three Matters* framework.

The first aspect of the framework is a Strong Child, the components of which – Me Myself and I, Being Acknowledged and Affirmed, Developing Self-assurance and A Sense of Belonging – all relate to the meeting of the first fundamental human need: the need to feel at home and confident in the environment, that is, to feel a 'goodness-of-fit'.

The second aspect of the framework is a Skilful Communicator. Within this aspect occur such issues as babies acting to communicate, babies experimenting and exploring, adults making a game of everyday activities – all relating to the second basic human need to act on, that is, explore and influence, the environment.

A Competent Learner, the third aspect, includes features such as mirroring, modelling, imagining, drawing on resources and making connections. All reflect our third great need to carry through new ideas, passing them on as we connect them to those of others.

The fourth aspect, a Healthy Child, beautifully expresses the expanded base of trust and confidence that relaunches the developmental needs model when the first three needs are met: 'When young children have a close relationship with a caring and responsive adult, they explore from a safe place to which they can return' (DfES 2002).

In this chapter we will see that when parents have a relationship with caring and responsive others at home, in the childcare centre or elsewhere, they too explore from a safe place to which they can return and from which they can relaunch.

The proposed framework, relating to both adults and children, in brief, suggests that as we attempt to meet our fundamental needs we often require help. As other people help us to meet these needs, we build up our stock of internal resources. If we start from what Ainsworth (1967) called a 'secure base', that is, we are confident that when we need support someone is there for us, a goodness-of-fit exists between ourselves and our immediate environment. When others help us to meet our need to feel that goodness-of-fit with our environment, we build our internal resource of trust. When others help us to meet our need to explore and influence the variety of that environment, we build our internal resource of autonomy. When they help us to meet our need to replicate and exchange new ideas from the insights we have gained about the environment, we build our internal resource of initiative. Thus we reach a new, extended 'secure base' from which these three processes can operate again and again and again, all through our lives.

What is important to note is that the fulfilment of these needs and the acquisition of their outcomes – trust autonomy and initiative (Erikson 1950) – are developmental. It is not possible to build up new ideas in a field before one has come to feel reasonably at home in it, and has discovered some of its many characteristics. Indeed 'babies need acceptance' that is independent of their behaviour; it is acceptance without reservations and without judgements' (Roberts 2002: 5); only then can they reach their full potential and the same is true of adults.

Meeting our developmental needs – adults and children interacting

The QUT study

I and a team of researchers in the Queensland University of Technology (QUT) School of Early Childhood wanted to see whether, as young children and their parents engage in the everyday activities they constantly carry out round the house, the children are getting help from their parents in meeting their developmental needs. At the same time we also wanted to find out to what extent such everyday activities with their children helped parents to meet their own developmental needs (Broughton *et al.* 1999). These findings about parents and their children are a major focus of this chapter.

We embarked on the study because we suspected that in the course of these activities there are processes occurring which have until recently been largely overlooked by researchers investigating development (except in a few studies, e.g. Rheingold 1982; Tizard and Hughes 1984; Rogoff 1990). Our study, which took place over several years, followed 29 adult-child pairs (17 girls, 12 boys) engaged in four everyday activities. The children were video-taped with their parent or carer annually until they reached the age of 4. Each child's interactions with the adult or peers were videotaped as they engaged in normal activities such as looking at books, playing with toys, eating or preparing food, or putting on or taking off clothes.

These interactions between adult and child were analysed for the focus and length of each interaction, including details such as who had initiated and terminated it. In addition, questionnaires were distributed and the adults (parents or carers/teachers) answered open-ended questions about their own and their child's likes and dislikes about the four everyday activities under consideration. From these data, we began to establish whether and how both the children and their parents were meeting their developmental needs as they engaged in these activities, and the resources necessary for their fulfilment.

Young children meeting their developmental needs through everyday activities with adults

The findings showed that:

- children enjoyed taking part in these everyday activities, spending at least three-quarters of their time with their parents in this way;
- at all ages the child's choice predicted the activity, with the child initiating, or the parent following and responding to the child's focus, though over time the length of parent-directed sequences in-creased;
- as the children grew and developed from 12 to 36 months, they attempted to prolong their interactions with parents, whilst parents increasingly curtailed them;
- boys took longer to reach their peak of interaction, while their mo-thers, relative to the girls' mothers, grew more directive and didactic as time went on.

Translating these findings into children's developmental needs, it is clear that the children:

- were meeting their need for goodness-of-fit, feeling comfortable – indeed increasingly comfortable – as they engaged with their parent or carer in everyday activities;
- were meeting their need to explore and influence their surroundings as their own focus prevailed in these everyday activities, though this autonomy, especially for the boys, was increasingly curtailed;

- were meeting their need to replicate new ideas acquired from others as the length of parent-directed sequences increased over time.

To varying degrees, these Strong Children (affirming their sense of belonging) were becoming Skilful Communicators (acting to communicate, explore and influence) and Competent Learners (drawing on resources and making connections). It appeared that the extent to which they had a 'relationship with a caring and responsive adult' related closely to their development as a Healthy Child.

Adults meeting their developmental needs through everyday activities with young children

The needs of the parents and carers/practitioners were clearly revealed by the responses to the questionnaire that adult participants willingly completed. Parents, in particular, were eager to write at length in answer to the questions we asked. Examples of these included:

- What do you like about looking at books with X?
- What do you like about playing with toys with X?
- What do you like about preparing food for/with X?
- What do you like about changing clothes with X?

And conversely, the questions 'What don't you like about ... ?' were also asked.

Adults meeting their developmental needs through everyday activities with children – building trust

A major finding of the study was that for the 1-year-olds and their parents it was not only the children who enjoyed these everyday activities. This picture of enjoyment has not been the one reflected in much of the literature. Belsky (1988: 279) writes that early parenthood is stressful – 'and for a variety of reasons: babies cry, need a great deal of attention and must be fed in the middle of the night'. But two-thirds of our respondents wrote glowingly of their pleasure at taking part in activities with their very young children (Gahan 1994). Our videotaped record confirms that three-quarters of the parents' time – equal of course to that of the children – was spent in such interaction. In part, of course, we are genetically programmed for such a reaction (Alley 1983). The fact that many adults enjoy interacting with babies underlies a remarkable finding from a study by Carpenter et al. (1998) concerning the foundation of infants' beginning language skills. Long before infants start to burble, tweet and chortle to someone else (at about 15 months), these authors have reported on the behaviour of a number of mothers and their babies of 9 months participating in 'joint attentional engagement' (1998: 113). In terms of the model being advanced in this chapter, this means both baby and mother meeting their initial need to feel comfortable with each other. How do they do this? By sharing attention. As soon as a baby is born, mother and baby are able to look at each other. At 9 months (the point at which the study began) they are sharing attention round an object. Mother and baby look, for example, at a mobile, then at each other, then back at the mobile, then back at each other. Mothers do this because, as described above, they love to spend time and to be in touch (literally) with their baby. And babies? As noted by Baldwin and Moses (1996), faced with some unfamiliar object or novel event, infants 'stay close to, and are especially willing to interact with, someone with whom they feel entirely at ease' (p. 1925). For both mother and baby, joint attentional engagement round a novel object (the mobile) in the presence of the most familiar object in their world – for the mother the baby, for the baby the mother (or sometimes father or carer) – allows both of them to feel increasingly at home with each other and so build up trust.

In the QUT study not all parents so wholeheartedly met their own need to feel comfortable and to build trust and satisfaction with their babies (Gahan 1994). While, in their questionnaire responses, 66 per cent of the parents recorded their pleasure in social interaction with their child, for some there was clear evidence of mixed feelings. Gahan notes that over four-fifths of mothers of girls wrote of their enjoyment:

- 'I love the way she instantly sits back in my arms when I convey to her that a story is about to be read.'
- 'She sometimes shows prolonged concentration, seems to anticipate the bits she likes, dances to nursery rhymes, snuggles up, and becomes interactive.'

But the predominant expression from mothers of boys (again over four-fifths) was one of frustration:

- 'I have given up trying to read or even point out pictures in a book. I'm happy now even if we just sit and he chews the page. I know, in time, he will enjoy them as books to be read.'
- 'It's frustrating trying to dress a moving target.'

In a later section of this chapter, we will look at reasons for this gender difference.

Adults meeting their developmental needs through everyday activities with children – building autonomy

In our findings of the children's interactions with their parents, we noted that for several years the child's focus prevailed, either the child initiating or the parent following in to the child's focus. This predominance of the child's focus in over 50 per cent of total interactions occurred at 12, 24 and 36 months for both boys and girls. Tomasello and Farrar (1986) identified this as a key element in children's learning, that is, 'allowing a joint attentional sequence to be coordinated immediately, whereas adult redirection of the child's focus demands of the child an attention-switching strategy' (McDonell 2000: 3).

Parents' willingness to follow their child's lead was not only confined to their interactions. There were also periods of non-interactive, solo parental activity that we labelled 'onlooking'. Onlooking parents observed their children who were independently attending to something else. Three-quarters of these onlooking episodes were followed by a return to interaction; of these returns, 'two-thirds were constructed round the child's focus' (McDonell 2000: 3). This raises the question whether, in choosing to follow the child's lead, parents are retaining their autonomy or being dominated by their 'strong' children.

Ainsworth *et al.* (1974: 107) argue for the former: by enlarging their sphere of action the parent is able to 'work with the grain of her baby's repertoire, rather than against it'. As the baby constantly changes (so that parents too have to change their behaviour), it is a new world that the parent is exploring, along with the baby. As they look into each other's eyes in joint engagement, and later, as the parent attends to the baby's pointings, burblings and summonings, there is always something unexpected for the adult (as well as the baby) to discover. Parents' 'following in' is one area of adult autonomy.

Carpenter *et al.* (1998: 113) identified that 'mothers' tendency to use language to follow into their infant's attentional focus' is a major process associated with infant language skills at 15 months, a further significant process being the amount of time spent in joint engagement. This maternal 'following in' occurred when the babies were about 10 to 11 months of age, in Carpenter's sample. It is the extent of parents' involvement in infants' ability to understand language several months later that Carpenter *et al.* call 'an amazing outcome' of their study. They found that, in predicting infants' early language skills, parental involvement accounted for over half the variance 'with basically two measures of social interaction – one of the tendency of mother-infant dyads to enter into joint attentional engagement and one of mothers' tendency to use language to follow into the infant's attentional focus' (1998: 113).

Our study confirmed the importance of these findings and as in Carpenter's study showed that mothers were meeting their own needs:

- first to feel at home as they built trust by engaging with their baby for three-quarters of their time;
- next to explore a new world, building their own autonomy by following into what was interesting the baby!

But for adults there is a tension here – the tension of real life. The same tension appears in the description of humans' need to explore/influence the environment. As change occurs, organisms both explore and influence their immediate environment. Exploring and influencing are both attempts to 'do our own thing'. Both are demonstrations of human autonomy, yet they are often in conflict.

Parents have a broader immediate environment than their babies. Babies' environment consists of their parents and the activities they and their parents perform. But for parents, their immediate environment comprises not only their babies but also events to do with the household, the family, money, shopping, other people, education issues, employment issues and community issues. Life must go on, and it is not surprising that our study found parents, over time, curtailing their interactions with their young children, even as the children attempted to prolong those interactions. With these competing demands on them, no wonder many parents' responses, in their questionnaires, expressed frustration. Yet there are times when the tension, for adults, associated with two opposing manifestations of autonomy related to their young children, can be resolved. Sometimes we can simultaneously explore *and* influence.

So the description by Gahan (1994: 2) of a 12-month-old baby girl sitting on her mother's knee singing with her mother 'See saw Marjorie Daw' while changing socks is an example of 'parents' concern to enliven food and clothing routines with diversionary games and jingles'. Mother is pushing on with the daily chores of dressing (influencing her environment) while giving herself as well as her baby fun (exploring a new musical game) as she rocks and sings.

While being purposeful and predictable, family activities are also flexible, allowing for dynamic variations in participation (McNaughton 1995). As adult-child negotiation within and about an activity occurs, the child's individual characteristics influence adult guidance strategies resulting in the ongoing development of both adult and child participants (Rogoff 1990; Valsiner and Winegar 1992). Not only the child, but also the adult, through the child, is meeting the fundamental human need both to explore and influence. On these occasions, both parent and child are building autonomy, as Broughton (1998) puts it, with 'purposeful and predictable' but also 'flexible' and 'dynamic' variations in participation.

Adults meeting their developmental needs through everyday activities with children – building initiative

Becoming aware, or gaining understanding of something, is deeply satisfying for all of us. It is indeed the building of initiative. As illustrated in the last section, we need, whether we are children or adults, to explore and influence our immediate environment, acquiring insights as we do so. These insights result in new ideas which we need to pass on, sharing them with others – through modelling and language. Everyday activities at home offer parents this opportunity. While, in our QUT study, the exploratory (child-directed) sequences continued to prevail, parent-directed sequences became longer over time. Broughton (1998) notes that as age increased, children were increasingly able to sustain attention to parent- or teacher-directed foci, reflecting an increasing ability to maintain intersubjectivity (Bruner 1983). These abilities are foundational for cultural participation and learning in contexts beyond the family.

Whether we are 3, 33 or 83, intersubjective abilities remain foundational for cultural participation. Adults are pre-programmed for such intersubjectivity – that is, being on the same wavelength as another and knowing it. This would account for what otherwise might be considered very strange parent behaviour. Parents first spend 'a significant amount of time' (Carpenter *et al.* 1998: 109) sharing attention with a baby, then they follow into the baby's focus, then they engage in a language duet with an apprentice baby speaker (McGurk 1986). Why do they do this? Because they feel 'at home'; they have goodness-of-fit with their environment, and they are able both to explore and influence it. Finally, as their baby grows, they can increasingly meet their need to share themselves and their ideas with 'someone with whom they feel entirely at ease' (Baldwin and Moses 1996: 1925).

Gender differences and parents' responses to children

It appears, then that, unless negative environmental factors intervene, both adults and children have a genetic predisposition to collaborate in meeting their developmental need to share ideas, building the internal resource of initiative as they do so. As with the fulfilment of the first two needs, however, the QUT study has shown that in our sample the parental need to share ideas was met variably, its fulfilment affected along gender lines.

Gahan's (1994) summary of the parents' questionnaire responses when their children were 12 months old showed that, even at this early age, the use of books and toys was seen by parents to have cultural and educational value, while clothing and food were seen as caretaking activities, which parents attempted to make interesting by incorporating games and diversions. Based on whether they had a boy or a girl, parents in our sample reacted differently to these two sets of activities. In the case of boys, 77 per cent of mothers referred to the value of books as tools for learning (compared with 54 per cent of mothers of girls). Mothers of boys also more often expressed a desire and concern for their child to mature in terms of attention span with books, while mothers of girls did not mention this in the context of book-reading routines, their comments being much more descriptive of the social context in which the book-reading took place. A marked didactic approach to reading with their child was evident in comments by mothers of boys:

- 'I love asking him questions about the objects in the books. He regularly gives correct answers – very rewarding.'
- 'I like to see if I get a response to a picture. It may be a familiar object to him.'
- 'I like him knowing the names of objects and seeing him growing up, for example becoming interested in staying longer.'

In contrast, mothers of girls specifically focused on their mutual enjoyment of the intimacy engendered by reading books together. For example:

- 'I love the special times alone – when only that child is present – like book-reading.'
- 'Having her want to sit with you to read and have her respond to you when reading.'
- 'My child loves to be held and read to.'

Toy play was accompanied by similar parental approaches. While the social aspects of such play were mentioned by 87 per cent of mothers of girls but only 55 per cent of mothers of boys, the teaching/learning aspects of toy play virtually reversed these proportions. The importance of learning through toys was mentioned by 53 per cent of mothers of girls and 77 per cent of mothers of boys. Despite the frustration levels of toy play mentioned by mothers of boys, for all the 12-month-old boys who engaged in it, toy play was initiated by parents with their own (directive) focus (Gahan 1994).

Throughout the chapter we have seen that in relation to the need for goodness-of-fit and the outcome of trust, while there was an overall substantial enjoyment of the children by parents, and while both parents and children chose to spend at least three-quarters of their time doing things together, parents of boys expressed considerably more frustration with their behaviour than did parents of girls.

In relation to the need to explore/manipulate the changing environment and build autonomy, it is not surprising that the less mature and more active boys took longer to achieve their interactional peak (reaching it at 3 years whereas the more mature girls achieved this peak at 2). During these years all the children were attempting to prolong their interactions with parents, while parents – with other things on their minds – were increasingly terminating them. More mature girls may cope more readily with this, whereas boys may experience further frustration.

This may help to account for a fascinating finding in the QUT study relating to the third great human need to exchange and replicate ideas, and thus build initiative. We identified other themes (beyond the four everyday activities) that occupied the parents and children. One of these was 'conversation' – which included any vocal interchange. As described in the Karitane Report (Henry *et al.* 1999: 14), at 12 months and 24 months 'conversational' sequences between boys and their parents were as long (longer indeed, but not significantly so) as those between the girls and their parents. But by 36 months the boys' conversations with parents were significantly shorter than the girls', and remained so at 54 months. Since young girls have long been credited with superior verbal skills (Reznick and Goldfield 1992), this finding relating to the falling away by age 3 of boys' very early competence merits further investigation.

Perhaps linked to this was the finding in our study that the view held of their children by the majority of parents replicated worldwide social stereotypes. Most parents of girls saw them as expressive, warm and responsive rather than achievement-oriented. Most parents of boys, whose learning has been stereotyped as instrumentally focused on achievement and earning a living (Williams and Best 1982), saw them as dominant, rational beings who must be assisted to learn (even at 12 months). The investigating team at QUT (Broughton *et al.* 1999) pondered whether these parents were reacting to child competence and level of development, or whether they were inculcating stereotypical perspectives of male and female roles (Ruble and Ruble 1982). Indeed they might have been responding to both.

Whatever the answers to these questions, Berk (1994: 551) suggests that rather than the differences between boys and girls, it is the similarities that need emphasizsing:

> Although biological factors are involved in some differences, they make it only slightly easier for one sex to acquire certain attributes. Both boys and girls can learn all of them, and families, schools and peers affect the size of each difference. Our overall conclusion must be that males and females are much more alike in developmental potential than they are different from each other.

Summarizing this section, it is clear that numbers of parents in this study are meeting – but often only partially – their own needs through their relationships with their children. Parents often seem to be forcing both themselves and their sons forward to comply with the third element of a model of developmental needs, the extension of ideas, before the first two elements, the building of trust and autonomy, have been affirmed. We may speculate on the long-term patterns of resentfulness between men and women in adult society which these mutually frustrating relationships between mothers and their sons may in part underlie. At the same time, little girls may still, across the whole of society, be missing out on the encouragement to achieve which many of the parents of boys in our study were unduly promoting.

Yet the strongest finding in our study remains the basic enjoyment which boys, girls and their parents all found in choosing to do things together for three-quarters of their time. How can parents and carers consolidate their delight in this evolutionary goodness-of-fit, ensuring that the little boys they are caring for acquire a sense of loving intimacy, the little girls a sense of achievement? To look for solutions we turn to the source of help we adults always have at our disposal: other adults like ourselves.

Meeting our own developmental needs through everyday activities – adults interacting with other adults

Just as parents and carers/teachers can help young children fulfil their developmental needs, so adults can help one another in similar ways (Henry 2004). First, by interacting responsively with each other, we adults can help each other to feel goodness-of-fit with our environment. Next, by exploring and influencing that environment together, we acquire a variety of insights which we can pass on, as ideas, sharing them through ongoing communication with each other. Thus interacting adults (e.g. parents and carers/ teachers) build up our internal resources of trust, autonomy and initiative.

Key to each phase of the meeting of these developmental needs is the interaction between organism and immediate environment. We have seen in a previous section that parents have a more complex environment than their infants. Within such an environment, how can parents collaborate with other adults so they can better meet their developmental needs in relation to their young children? To meet their first need (feeling goodness-of-fit with their children), and their second need (exploring and influencing the child's world) the solution is obvious, if not easy. It is for parents to take more time doing these things. For this to happen, parents may require more cooperation from other adults. Sources might be other family members, for example, fathers (Russell 1994), individual community members as in the Home Start programme (Harrison 2003), and legislators creating more family-friendly work practices, childcare and parental leave provisions. Such supports would help to provide precisely what Carpenter *et al.* have shown is necessary for parents and infants to meet their first two developmental needs, 'a significant amount of time' (1998: 109).

Parents' third developmental need requires a different solution. Relating to this need and its outcome (initiative, the carrying through of ideas) are the different attitudes to males and females shown in our study. In grappling with this third need, parents would gain from having more opportunities to share ideas with other adults interested in behaviours helpful to young children. In the QUT study the participating carers/teachers, in part perhaps because of their training, with its extensive exploratory focus on the child's world, have been described earlier in this chapter as keeping interactions going for long periods, following in massively to the focus of both boys and girls. Such carers/teachers could also help to meet the developmental needs of parents. More one-to-one contacts as well as discussion groups involving early educators and parents, in which all participants acquire confidence in exchanging ideas with one another, would make it more likely that in their everyday activities with young children both sets of adults would increasingly build up their own resources of trust, autonomy and initiative. These internal resources apply to all of us, male and female, and with their increase the notions of expressiveness for girls and instrumentality for boys might come to appear nonsensically restrictive, since, as already quoted: 'Our overall conclusion must be that males and females are much more alike in developmental potential than they are different from each other' (Berk 1994: 551). All need loving intimacy; all need to act and achieve.

Not only parents would benefit from exchanging ideas with carers/teachers about helpful behaviours. Carers and teachers would equally benefit from exchanging ideas with parents. As Nimmo has pointed out, our formal early childhood settings should 'include the range of family-related everyday experiences' (1986: 11) which are far too few in our institutions and on which parents are authorities. Bronfenbrenner (1994: 67) has called for the adoption in our educational institutions of a 'curriculum for caring'. The parents in the QUT study had plenty of suggestions to offer.

Can parents (as well as children) meet their developmental needs through everyday activities?

The QUT study has shown through its most powerful finding that a curriculum for caring lies at the heart of family life, despite the difficulties in implementing it. That finding is that both parents and very young children enjoy carrying out everyday activities together and spend a major proportion of their time doing so. With varying degrees of success the parent is playing a major part in creating a Strong Child, a Skilful Communicator, a Competent Learner and a Healthy Child. As parents collaborate with other adults round their child's concerns, they will increase their own internal resources of trust, autonomy and initiative. By meeting their own needs more fully they will have still more to bring to their children.

REFERENCES

Ainsworth, M.D.S. (1967) *Infancy in Uganda: Infant Care and the Growth of Love.* Baltimore, MD: Johns Hopkins Press.

Ainsworth, M.D.S., Bell, S.M. and Stayton, D.J. (1974) Mother-infant interaction and the development of competence, in K.J. Connolly and J.S. Bruner (eds) *The Growth of Competence.* New York: Academic Press.

Alley, T. (1983) Growth-produced changes in body shape and size as determinants of perceived age and adult caregiving, *Child Development,* 54: 241–8.

Baldwin, D.A. and Moses, L.J. (1996) The ontogeny of social information gathering, *Child Development,* 67(5): 1915–39.

Belsky, J. (1988) Child maltreatment and the emergent family system, in K. Browne, C. Davies and P. Stratton (eds) *Early Prediction and Prevention of Child Abuse.* Chichester: John Wiley.

Berk, L.E. (1994) Child Development, 3rd edn. Boston, MA: Allyn & Bacon.

Bronfenbrenner, U. (1994) A new head start for Head Start, *New Horizons in Education,* 91(December): 57–70.

Broughton, B. (1998) The significance of everyday experiences in the lives of young children. Paper presented at l'Organisation Mondiale d'Education Prescolaire, Copenhagen, August.

Broughton, B., Henry, M.B., McDonell, J. and Gahan, D. (1999) Joint attention sequences: key findings from the longitudinal study. Presentation to the Centre for Applied Studies in Early Childhood, Brisbane.

Bruner, J.S. (1957) On going beyond the information given, in *Cognition: The Colorado Symposium.* Cambridge, MA: Harvard University Press.

Bruner, J.S. (1983) *Child's Talk: Learning to Use Language.* New York: Norton.

Carpenter, M., Nagell, K. and Tomasello, M. (1998) *Social Cognition, Joint Attention and Communicative Competence from 9–15 Months of Age.* Monograph of the Society for Research in Child Development, 63(4). Chicago: University of Chicago Press.

DfES (2002) *Birth to Three Matters.* London: DfES Publications.

Edgar, D. (1993) Competence in children, *Family Matters,* 36(December): 7–10.

Erikson, E. (1950) *Childhood and Society.* New York: Norton.

Field, T.M. (1977) Effects of early separation, interactive deficits, and experimental manipulation on infant-mother face-to-face interaction, *Child Development,* 48: 763–71.

Gahan, D. (1994) Infant development in the context of everyday activities. Paper presented at the Twentieth Triennial Conference of the Australian Early Childhood Association, Perth, October.

Harrison, M. (2003) *Hooray! Here Comes Tuesday: The Home-Start Story.* Leicester: Bamaha.

Henry, M.B. (2004) Developmental needs and early childhood education: evolutionary, my dear Watson, *Early Child Development and Care*, 174(4): 301–12.

Henry, M.B., Broughton, B., Gahan, D. and McDonell, J. (1999) *Report to Karitane on the Significance of Shared Everyday Activities in Facilitating Young Children's Development.* Brisbane: Centre for Applied Studies in Early Childhood, QUT.

McDonell, J. (2000) Early learning in adult-child joint attentional sequences. Paper presented at the International Conference on Infant Studies, Brighton UK, July.

McGurk, H. (1986) Introductory address, in B. Raward and J. Ferguson (eds) *Early Childhood: Ideals/Realities.* Canberra: Australian Early Childhood Association.

McNaughton, S. (1995) *Patterns of Emergent Literacy: The Process of Development and Transition.* Melbourne: Oxford University Press.

Nimmo, J. (1986) Unique curricula for day care: considerations for future directions, *Australian Journal of Early Childhood*, 11(1): 10–14.

Reznick, J.S. and Goldfield, B.A. (1992) Rapid change in lexical development in comprehension and production, *Developmental Psychology*, 28: 406–13.

Rheingold, H.L. (1982) Little children's participation in the work of adults, a nascent prosocial behaviour, *Child Development*, 53: 114–25.

Roberts, R. (2002) *Developing Self-Esteem in Young Children.* London: Paul Chapman/Sage.

Rogoff, B. (1990) *Apprenticeship in Thinking: Cognitive Development in Social Context.* New York: Oxford University Press.

Ruble, D.N. and Ruble, T.L. (1982) Sex stereotypes, in A.G. Miller (ed.) *In the Eye of the Beholder.* New York: Praeger.

Russell, G. (1994) Sharing the pleasures and pains of family life, *Family Matters*, 37(April): 13–19.

Tanner, J.M. (1990) *Foetus into Man*, 2nd edn. Cambridge, MA: Harvard University Press.

Tizard, B. and Hughes, M. (1984) *Young Children Learning: Talking and Thinking at Home and at School.* London: Fontana.

Tomasello, M. and Farrar, M.J. (1986) Joint attention and early development, *Child Development*, 57: 1454–63.

Valsiner, J. and Winegar, L.T. (eds) (1992) *Children's Development Within Social Context.* Hillsdale, NJ: Lawrence Erlbaum.

Williams, J.E. and Best, D.L. (1982) *Measuring Sex Stereotypes: A Thirty-Nation Study.* Beverley Hills, CA: Sage.

5 'Don't You Tell Me What to Do'

Helen Moylett and Kim Holyman

This chapter is about working with parents when the going gets tough: when relationships and boundaries are tested to their limits and when practitioners and parents may find it hard to remember that the welfare of the children is their priority. We have both worked with children and families in a variety of contexts and we draw on a range of situations here, but mainly on our recent experience working together in an early years centre – Helen as the head and Kim as the manager responsible for the under 3s.

At the centre there are 20 places and two rooms for children under 3. The rooms are connected by a bathroom and shared messy area and children move between them and also into the outdoor area and the much larger over 3s nursery when appropriate. All the children under 3 are referred by social services and/or health – they are all children 'in need' as defined by the Children Act 1991. This is because demand for places far exceeds those available, and the neediest children have to be given priority. Clearly this means that their families may also be very needy and that some of the under 3s are looked-after children – staff may be working with foster carers as well as birth parents.

This situation presents various challenges for the practitioners, for the children themselves and for their parents, not just in the under 3s rooms, but as they progress through the centre. The centre is a learning community for children, staff and parents, and all staff are involved in a range of support programmes and initiatives to help families and other carers (Moylett and Djemli 2005). The centre has been working with *Birth to Three Matters* (DfES 2002) since its inception (Moylett and Holyman 2005) and all parents and carers are involved in discussions about their children using the framework. All staff are qualified to at least NVQ 3 level.

Clearly we will be focusing on the centre's work with the very youngest children but the rest of the team also contribute to the centre ethos and the ways in which children, parents and carers are included and valued[1]. This chapter is a tribute to all of them and the children, parents and carers with whom they work.

---

[1] Thanks to Janet Thomas, current Head of Tamworth Early Years Centre, for her support in allowing us to write this chapter.

Working with parents

It is important to recognize that, although we are focusing here on the times when things get difficult, these difficulties take place in the context of a centre which has a strong ethos of inclusion and which is successful in working with parents. The centre, like the vast majority of other early years settings, provides a range of opportunities for parental involvement. For example, parents are always welcome to drop in, they contribute to their children's profiles, they work in the centre as volunteers and progress to qualifications. There are the usual courses, workshops and family learning sessions. These are always informal and hands-on, and parents are asked what they want. Most parents are keen to help their children in any way they can and appreciate opportunities to try out activities, both as an adult group and with their children. Parents and carers also join in cross-centre initiatives like emotional well-being for adults and children, working with an artist or improving the outdoor area. This just gives a flavour of what happens – there is not space here to go into detail about all the ways in which positive relationships with parents are built.

However, we believe that in working with parents, as with so many other relationships, it is not so much what happens but *how* it happens that matters. Effective communication is the key to successfully building relationships between staff and parents (Hughes and MacNaughton 2002). It is important, for instance, that parents understand centre philosophy and practice and that *Birth to Three Matters* and the *Curriculum Guidance for the Foundation Stage* (QCA/DfEE 2000) are de-mystified, but it is also just as important that they feel that they are listened to and can contribute their ideas, and are not patronized or treated as if they were at school. So staff need to really believe and practice the statement in the centre inclusion policy which says that 'Inclusion is a process which runs through the whole curriculum for all children and also affects all the adults – staff, parents and visitors'. The centre handbook states that the centre recognizes 'that family patterns differ and that children may live with one or both parents, with other relatives or carers, with gay or lesbian parents or in an extended family'. It also states that stereotyping of people on grounds of sex, race, class, sexuality or disability is challenged.

These values may be easier to practise in some circumstances than others. All of us bring our own baggage to our jobs. We may find it difficult to respect the needs of an addicted parent or to understand what certain parents are saying or the way they relate to their children or partners. These situations may reflect events in our own histories which we'd rather forget, or which may make us feel inadequate or angry. Sometimes we may feel that parents are not loving their children enough … but what does parental love mean?

Family patterns may differ, but when does different become dangerous? What is good enough parenting and what is neglect? These are just some of the questions that practitioners may find themselves asking. The ways in which they deal with them will be heavily dependent on their own values, experience and training, the support they get from their colleagues and the values and ethos of the centre.

In the next two sections we look at some of the ways in which practitioners working with children up to 3 years build relationships with parents and how boundary-setting can be very important in enabling questions like these to be answered for the benefit of children.

Building relationships

Before a child is admitted to the centre an admissions panel will have taken place where evidence from professionals involved with the family and from parents themselves, if they have asked for a centre place, is considered. Before the first home visit takes place centre staff know what other professionals' judgements are.

The home visit starts the process of building relationships and it is the first opportunity to discuss with parents/carers how the staff use *Birth to Three Matters*, the kinds of activities provided for children, how the key worker will observe their child in order to plan future activities and how parents can be involved. It is also an opportunity to watch parents and children interacting in their own home and for practitioners to form judgements about the attachment between them. Unless there is immediate cause for concern, these judgements are informal and unrecorded at this stage, but we all know the power of first impressions! Often during a home visit the parent will ask about social services involvement – particularly if they have been referred for parenting support as well as a place for their child. They may already be involved in child protection procedures and know that regular attendance at the centre and engagement in a parenting programme may help them keep their child. Practitioners are clear with parents about the child protection procedures and that if, after following these, senior staff are concerned that a child may be subject to any form of abuse, they are obliged to inform social services, but that this is done sensitively and confidentially and parents are kept informed.

Once the child starts at the centre an individual portfolio is started. This will hold information about the child from the parent(s) as well as observations that are made in the centre. These will be accompanied by photographs and descriptions or transcripts of the child's communications which help to give a picture of how the child has been involved in activities. There may also be examples of drawings, paintings or computer printouts. Children's achievements are celebrated through these individual profiles. They are shared with the parents and their contributions valued and included. Written summaries are made under the *Birth to Three Matters* aspects describing the child's achievements as well as identifying any particular support needed. If a child receives support in the centre from other professionals, such as the physiotherapist, this will also be included. This sharing of knowledge about the child is very important. As Langston and Abbott point out: 'As knowledge about a child is shared in a respectful way, value is placed on what parents know and this contributes to creating an ethos of acceptance and trust between the family and the day-care setting' (2005: 69).

Family Day occurs once per week. The centre minibus collects those who find travel to the centre difficult. Parents are able to take part in activities with their children, and staff are able to explain how what they are doing relates to *Birth to Three Matters*. It is an opportunity for parents to directly input information into their child's portfolio. This may be in the form of a photograph or information about what is going on at home, or family events they have been a part of, or it could be a description of what they have been involved in on Family Day. Family Days are generally attended by more mothers than fathers but efforts are always made to include significant males and 'men only' days are always well-attended and appreciated. The centre has only one male member of staff and it is easy to underestimate how difficult it can be for men to feel comfortable in what is seen as a female context.

Pat Djemli, who was formerly the care manager at the centre, writes about the benefits of Family Day for building trust and confidence between parents and practitioners as follows:

> As well as listening to parents, staff can share expertise informally on Family Day. Different stages of development can cause stress and tensions. Practitioners can offer advice and assistance to ease parents and children through these often emotive times such as meal times or toilet training. Knowing that what your child is demonstrating is a 'normal' part of a young child's development can be reassurance in itself. If it is cause for further concern the practitioner can offer advice and strategies for coping.
>
> (Moylett and Djemli 2005: 61)

Parents can take part in the organized group sessions within the Day that offer 'time out' from their children and where child health or adult issues are discussed. Sometimes just a friendly face and a listening ear is all that is needed for some families to enable them to confidently parent their children and to be reassured that it is 'normal' to sometimes find being a parent difficult and frustrating. By building and developing friendly professional relationships with families the aim is to create an environment where information or problems can be shared, without parents feeling they are being judged, and early intervention can prevent small problems escalating into big issues.

The trust and confidence in practitioners built up on Family Days can lead to parents asking for help and agreeing that the centre refer them to social services, and this preventative approach can avoid situations arriving at crisis point.

Establishing boundaries

We have stated earlier that relationships are informal. This may be seen in the relaxed and friendly greeting the secretary gives to parents and visitors, the ways in which staff talk to each other and the children, and in the way in which all staff are called by their first name. However, this does not mean that professional boundaries do not exist. Less experienced staff sometimes make the mistake of trying to be a friend to parents rather than a friendly professional. We feel that this distinction is very important.

As Rodd (2005: 253) asserts:

> Being an early childhood practitioner in contemporary society means more than being appropriately trained for and experienced in the care and education of young children. It means adopting a particular mental set or attitude towards one's work. Members of the field increasingly regard themselves as professionals, with a distinct professional identity and growing professional self esteem and confidence.

We believe that part of this mental set or attitude is not getting emotionally involved to the extent that one forgets the need we mentioned earlier: for practitioners to translate policy into practice in their work with all parents. A professional needs to be able to de-centre (focus on another's needs not their own) and respond rationally and helpfully. We support the view of the primary school head quoted in Strahan (1994: 160) 'No matter how a parent comes through that door – they may be screaming, they may be jumping up and down, you may know there's enormous problems, that they have come here to have a row, but my first approach is always "How can I help you?"'

That head had warm and friendly relations with parents but saw his professional role as a skilled helper or counsellor. When a parent is very distressed and angry and shouting 'Don't you tell me what to do' (or more offensive words to that effect) it is not helpful to them or oneself to either collude with them or shout back. Offering what Rogers (1951) referred to as 'unconditional positive regard' is important for anyone in distress and a refusal to be deflected by defensive behaviour, or be drawn into a row, often breaks into the negative self-defeating cycle that parents in difficult situations may set up. It then becomes possible for parents to become more coherent and begin to try and find ways forward for the benefit of their child.

Case study

In this case study we seek to show how some of the issues discussed in this chapter might occur and be dealt with by practitioners and parents. It draws on a variety of real incidents but they have been slightly changed and anonymized so that people cannot be identified directly.

David, aged 2.5 years, who has been referred by social services as a 'child in need', has been at the centre for six months. He regularly arrives late and is usually delivered by his mother, Julie. His father, Garry, very rarely comes to the centre. Julie usually says David's behaviour is the cause of their lateness, or claims that they have overslept because David and his siblings won't go to sleep at night, or that the youngest child has been sick, or that the car has broken down, or some other reason.

On this particular morning David arrives at the nursery at 9.40 a.m. with his mother. His key worker can see that David's clothes are dirty; that his face appears unwashed with black sticky marks around his mouth and cheeks; that he has purple felt pen marks on his hands and neck; and that his hair is very messy with headlice visible that David is scratching; his scalp looks scabby and sore. Julie pushes David into the room, where he remains motionless with his eyes fixed on the ground. Still standing in the doorway David's mother says, 'I know we're late, it's his fault, here you can have him'. She then leaves hurriedly saying that David's father is in the car waiting with the other children and that she has to go.

David is encouraged to come to the blanket on the floor where two other children are exploring the 'wooden collection'. He looks down at the floor, appearing rooted to the spot and does not make eye contact with anyone. Gina, David's key worker, knows that he really likes playing with the cars and so she invites him to come and help her get them out. No amount of persuasion will bring him to the blanket or to the cars and Gina places the basket of cars near to him. She sorts through them herself, describing each one, in the hope that she will tempt him to become engaged. By staying close by she is letting him know that she is there for him when he is ready. This has been a regular scenario during the beginning of the session and usually, after about 20 minutes, David starts to become more physically active.

Practitioners at the centre have regularly discussed David with Julie in a friendly professional way with a twofold aim:

- to support her in recognizing there may be problems that are impacting on David's welfare and that practitioners are there to help;
- to be open and honest about their concerns and share their observations and evidence.

This morning Gina has concerns for David's emotional and physical welfare based on her and other practitioners' observations regarding the following:

- David avoids eye contact or interaction with adults;
- David's hands, face and clothes are dirty and there is a smell of urine;
- David has headlice which has caused his scalp to bleed from his scratching;
- David's mother pushes him into the room, blaming David for the late arrival.

At other times Gina and others have also noticed:

- David only plays in isolation;
- David is constantly disruptive with peers' play;
- At 2.5 years David does not communicate verbally;
- David appears hungry on arrival at nursery and often grabs at the snack;
- David appears ambivalent when his mother returns to collect him.

Penn (2005: 114) discusses the work of Dunn, who studied young children growing up in families. Dunn suggested that 'children are highly responsive to the quality of relationships and emotional exchanges within the family'. Dunn went on to describe children as knowing 'when things are going wrong, even if they cannot voice their worries'. It seems to the practitioners that David is probably responding to the emotional and physical climate in the home, which seems to be damaging. His attachment to his mother seems weak and she does not appear to voice positive feelings for him.

Julie has been regularly invited to come to Family Day which would offer her the opportunity to be close to David away from home and, as we have pointed out elsewhere, would create opportunities for her to share special times 'that can have a marked effect on the parent-child relationship' (Moylett and Djemli 2005: 62). Julie would always say she was going to come to Family Day but never did. She would offer a range of reasons why it had not been possible.

While *Birth to Three Matters* is useful in helping the practitioner to celebrate the child's achievements, it can also support them in identifying problems. We can identify that David may not be having positive experiences to become:

A Healthy Child (as well as keeping safe):

- being special to someone;
- being able to express feelings;
- becoming aware of others and their needs;
- developing healthy dependence and independence.

A Strong Child:

- needing recognition, acceptance and comfort;
- feeling self-assured and supported;
- valuing individuality and contributions of self and others;
- having a role and identity within a group.

A Skilful Communicator:

- being with others;
- sharing thoughts and feelings;
- negotiating and making choices;
- gaining attention and making contacts.

A Competent Learner:

- imitating, mirroring moving and imagining;
- becoming playfully engaged and involved;
- finding out about the environment and other people.

Gina and her line manager decide that the time has come to have a more formal discussion with Julie about David's well-being and consider, if any, what further action should be taken. However, before any action is taken there are a number of issues to consider here:

- the risk factors for the child;
- the relationship between the parents and practitioners;
- the support needed for practitioners.

The Risk Factors for the Child

The main risk for the child here appears to be that David may be suffering abuse that will affect his development. There is always a risk that when a dialogue is started with parents about concerns, they take umbrage and stop the child from attending, which may intensify the abuse unless other forms of professional intervention are forthcoming. There is a risk that without intervention things will get worse for David.

Parent and Practitioner Relationships

We have to assume that parents want the best for their children and that when things do go wrong it is not generally a deliberate act on their part, but may be down to a number of factors that affect their skills at parenting. This is where the open, honest, friendly professional approach explained earlier in this chapter is very important.

It is our experience that the parent will often feel let down if child protection procedures are instigated. They may also be embarrassed and feel they are being judged as 'bad' parents. Sometimes a referral is made by the centre and does not result in any further investigation. This can leave the parent feeling very angry with the practitioners involved. It can even result in the parent removing the child or keeping them away for a while. It is in circumstances like these that the relationships and boundaries between practitioners and parents may be tested to their limits. It is the job of senior managers to support less experienced practitioners through these difficult conversations and take responsibility for the outcomes if appropriate.

Practitioner Support

Support for practitioners like Gina can take the form of conversations with line managers about possible ways to talk with Julie, about what the outcomes might be and how other agencies might be involved. These conversations might take place in performance review or supervision sessions or might be arranged specifically in relation to this situation. If Gina is relatively inexperienced, the line manager or another senior practitioner might take the lead in talking with Julie, and mentor Gina through the process as it unfolds.

This is what happened here. The conversation with Julie was led by Gina's manager who knows Julie very well. However, as she and Gina had predicted, Julie reacted very angrily and left shouting that her children were 'never coming near this ******* place again'. Before she left however, she was told gently and firmly that she was welcome to come back at any time and that a referral would be made to social services.

The social services referral led to all the children being considered as at risk of harm and they were taken into care. To assess if the parents would be able to adequately care for their children in the future, a parenting assessment programme was commissioned by the allocated social worker. This 12-week programme would be very structured and would be facilitated by Anne, an experienced senior nursery nurse, who the parents know from the centre. When the programme began Julie and Garry were initially hostile towards Anne. However, after discussing issues openly, they were persuaded that working in cooperation was the best course of action for themselves and their children.

As could be expected, there were many times throughout the programme when Julie and Garry were upset. It had been impossible to place any of the children together and so they were all in separate foster families. Therefore at most of the sessions the children were also upset, especially when they were parting from each other and their parents. This was of course also upsetting for Anne who needed to act in a professional and neutral way, while having empathy for the parents and children at these times. She was supported before and after sessions by her line manager and other colleagues.

The situation within the home and the home conditions had been found to be so concerning that, when the parenting programme was completed, it was recommended by both Anne and the social workers that further work be undertaken with the family before the children were returned home. There was still a long way to go for Julie and Garry and their children. However, the children were eventually placed back home in the care of their parents and the same practitioners as before cared for David at the centre.

What had changed? The family were accessing additional support from social services in caring for their children. The family situation was being monitored through the care plan under child protection procedures. The social worker recommended that the family attend Family Day, and the relationship between Gina and other staff and Julie and Garry was potentially even more stressful for them all. At this point practitioners needed additional support to talk through their feelings. Discussions took place about the child protection plans that had been made and about how to ensure the family would feel supported, valued and included in the care and education of their child while in the centre.

The staff continued to offer positive friendly professional relationships based on David's interests. At first Julie and Garry found it hard to respond, but a turning point came when, for the first time since David had started at the centre, his parents contributed to his portfolio. Julie chose a photograph. It showed Garry holding his 'gloop' covered hands up and David, with his own hands in the bowl, watching his dad. The observation read, 'David and his dad, Garry, enjoying exploring the "gloop" together, David said "grrug" as he squeezed his fingers through the gloop and, dad said "this feels all slimy – yuk"'. The entry in David's portfolio could have been described under many of the *Birth to Three Matters* aspects. This one was placed under a Skilful Communicator and the component of 'Being Together' which focuses on being a sociable and effective communicator including gaining attention and making contact, positive relationships, being with others and encouraging conversation.

Conclusion

Pugh *et al.* (1994: 65) quote a paediatrican:

There were times before I had my own children when I was already advising other people how to bring up theirs. I thought it was all really quite straightforward. These people who came to see me were in a mess. They weren't normal parents like we would be. And then we had children. And we were in a mess as well.

These words remind us how hard it is to parent, and how professional status and training do not necessarily make us better parents. However, professional status and training can make us better able to de-centre and help others to become better parents. Katz raises some interesting issues concerning the distinctions between parenting and teaching and talks about the need for practitioners to 'protect themselves from potential burnout by developing an optimal level of detached concern – optimum in terms of their own emotional stability and effective functioning' (1995: 169).

When parents are under stress and finding parenting difficult, practitioners are often going to need support to find the best ways forward for the children while maintaining respectful positive relationships with the parents and being clear about their own feelings and actions. In David's case *Birth to Three Matters*, clear child protection procedures and a strong ethos of inclusion based on shared values, supported all involved. When situations look impossible they can get better.

References

DfES (2002) *Birth to Three Matters*. London: DfES Publications.
Hughes, P. and MacNaughton, G. (2002) Preparing early childhood professionals to work with parents: the challenges of diversity and dissensus, *Australian Journal of Early Childhood*, 27(2): 14–20.
Katz, L. (1995) *Talks with Teachers of Young Children*. Norwood, NJ: Ablex.
Langston, A. and Abbott, L (2005) Quality matters, in L. Abbott and A. Langston (eds) *Birth to Three Matters*. Maidenhead: Open University Press.
Moylett, H. and Djemli, P. (2005) *Practitioners Matter*, in L. Abbott and A. Langston (eds) *Birth to Three Matters*. Maidenhead: Open University Press.
Moylett, H. and Holyman, K. (2005) We do it differently now. Paper presented at European Early Childhood Education Research Association Conference. Dublin, August 2005.

Penn, H. (2005) *Understanding Early Childhood Issues and Controversies*. Maidenhead: Open University Press.

Pugh, G., De'Ath, E. and Smith, C. (1994) *Confident Parents, Confident Children*. London: National Children's Bureau.

QCA/DfEE (2000) *Curriculum Guidance for the Foundation Stage*. London: QCA/DfEE.

Rodd, J. (2005) *Leadership in Early Childhood*, 3rd edn. Maidenhead: Open University Press.

Rogers, C.R. (1951) *Client Centred Therapy*. Boston, MA: Houghton Mifflin.

Strahan, H. (1994) 'You feel like you belong: establishing partnerships between parents and educators, in L. Abbott and R. Rodger (eds) *Quality Education in the Early Years*. Buckingham: Open University Press.

6 Parents and Child Protection Matter

John Powell

This chapter will explore the relationship that exists between parents, carers and different practitioners whose involvement has come about because of concerns relating to child protection.

The nature of the relationship that sometimes develops between parents and childcare services will be thoroughly explored and tensions, difficulties and issues will be examined. The difficulties that parents have in being perceived as positive, rather than failures, in child protection situations is often at the heart of problems of working in partnership and it is therefore important to consider the power dynamics that often result in child protection contexts. However, the chapter will also explore how some practitioners are able to overcome this difficulty by developing positive ways of working in partnership with parents which are more likely to effectively meet the needs of the very young child; and how the *Birth to Three Matters* framework (DfES 2002) can support this.

The current wave of initiatives arising from proactive government policy and resulting in easy access to childcare and an increase in Sure Start children centres with wrap-around care will be discussed. The ways in which centres develop effective policies and practices to prevent child abuse in partnership with parents and other practitioners will be examined as well as how issues arising are resolved.

The role of parents

Parents are highly significant beings in their children's lives and are responsible for providing the environment in which children will first experience the world. From their earliest moments in life children are developing their understanding from their experience within a variety of interactive and interpersonal contexts. Young children and babies learn through exploring the faces, associated sounds, smells and touches of their immediate caring adults who they have contact with. In many respects babies arrive already 'hard-wired' at birth with the equipment necessary to be able to respond to their carers but requiring regular interactive input to continue healthy development:

What is evident from neuroscience is that 'normal' brain development in early childhood is dependent upon environmental input and, for parents and carers, this means warm and loving, appropriate interaction with children who are living in a safe context in which they are nourished and nurtured and allowed opportunities to explore.

(David *et al.* 2003: 113)

The role of parents is extremely important and can sometimes appear daunting, particularly if the parents are new or isolated from their wider family or community and uncertain about what they should do as a new parent and who they should seek advice from about rearing their child(ren). The normative view of the new relationship between parents and a newborn baby suggests that it typifies a moment of 'unparalleled' opportunity for connection and interpersonal learning. A relationship is instigated and portrayed, and develops through a 'coming together' which involves learning about each other's characteristics, moods and personality traits. These are presented to each other through daily routines such as eating and playing and should lead to a greater sense of understanding of each other.

There are also legal ways of perceiving the responsibilities of parents to their children. The definition of 'parents' in contemporary UK society is diverse and complex. According to legal definition, parents are deemed to have responsibilities relating to their children which are set out in Section 3(1) of the Children Act 1989 as follows: 'parental responsibility means all the rights, duties, powers, responsibilities and authority which by law a parent of a child has in relation to the child and his property' (Powell 2001: 35). This legal definition shows that parents and their relationship to their children are clearly recognized in law and that there are expectations that parents, through the powers identified, will be in the best place to care for them. There are therefore no simple assumptions about their role but a set of specific and legally binding statements that locate parents within a discourse that emphasizes responsibility and accountability. However, Powell argues that parental responsibilities can almost be considered as types of commodities to be 'traded between parents' (2001: 35), particularly in cases where parental relationships have become unravelled and negotiation about the parts that parents may play after divorce are discussed. The responsibility for the care of children and what care may be constituted as tends often to be viewed as a cultural dynamic and perceived not solely as existing within the domain of parents but also to have a strong societal dimension. In this sense while parents and their responsibilities are seen as constructed through legal definition, wider society is also recognized for the part that it plays in helping to shape a more 'living' set of values that relate to conforming to a general view of 'acceptable' parent and child practices, and whether they appear to be within community norms for what is expected as 'responsible'. This way of viewing parents' responsibilities as a construction of the wider community also links with UK government's policy set out in *Every Child Matters* which identifies an increased number of Sure Start children's centres which are expected to 'play a key role in communities alongside schools and general practitioners (GPs) as a focus for parents and children to access services' (HM Treasury 2003: 26). Parents come into contact in such centres with a range of practitioners as a matter of routine, from the day their children are born and even before birth. For example, parents may access health services through attendance at antenatal classes to prepare them for the birth, and later they may receive a visit from the health visitor following the birth. In addition parents may be seen at home so that the new baby can be given a health check by their GP on return from hospital. Later a primary health assessment may be completed for both the mother and baby by a health visitor at home. Other developmental checks are also likely to be taking place in the baby's early life and parents are likely to be offered immunization for their baby.

Parents may also make contact with other childcare services in a range of situations from the birth of the child. These services are wide-ranging and can be accessed by parents through voluntary, independent and statutory providers such as childminders, au pairs, nurseries and Sure Start children centres. Parents are likely to be able to gain admission to these different forms of childcare provision as a means of supporting re-entry into employment or to provide a breathing space. Parents could be taking their children to some form of early childcare provision before there are any formal requirements for them to do so at the age of 5 when children are statutorily required to attend school. Young children and their parents are therefore likely in contemporary society to have contact with a number of carers outside their immediate family. To this extent children can be viewed as a co-construction and shared responsibility between parents and any professional practitioners who share their care, plus immediate and wider family and members of the community. Usually the relationship that exists between parents and their children's carers is a relaxed and trusting one as both the family and the practitioners are likely to share the same kind of interests to promote the potential of each child.

However, the relationship with carers can change dramatically where concerns are raised that a child may be suffering in some way and particularly when this includes some form of ill-treatment. In such a situation a diverse range of practitioners concerned with child protection may become involved and concerns may be expressed about the ability of parents to care for their children.

For the sake of this chapter the term 'parent' refers to a generalized concept that incorporates the notion of a person acting as mother, father or guardian, and the parent may be in a relationship with a partner of opposite or same sex or bringing up their child singly. Parents may be living together or apart or in a relationship with someone who is not a birth parent. In addition the relationship between partners may be problematic and in some cases outwardly hostile.

It is unsurprising therefore that the pressures that parents may experience can lead to a situation where overreaction or frustration can result in a child being harmed:

> It is recognized that many families are under considerable stress, that being a parent is hard work, and families have a right to expect practical support from universal services, such as health and educa-tion. The importance of all parents having available to them good quality local resources is acknowledged.
>
> (DoH 2000: 1)

In order to consider the possible experiences that parents may have in child protection situations, the following case study is offered to help as a focus for discussion.

Case study

Family details:
Susan A, age 25, shop worker
Peter D, age 30, labourer
Benjamin A, age 5, attending Smiles Children Centre
Sasha A, age 2.5, attending Smiles Children Centre
Ingrid D, 10 weeks

The family live in a deprived area of an urban conurbation in a terraced three-bedroomed house which they rent from a private landlord. Susan has a strong network of friends and relatives who all live in the neighbourhood. However, Peter comes from another part of the country and tends to have separate friends from Susan. Susan's wider family appears to be close-knit and protective of its members.

Susan has worked for the past six months at a major retail store after the local children's centre agreed to admit Benjamin and Sasha, at the request of the social services department, to the day nursery a year ago. Susan had completed an IT course at the children's centre which helped her to get the job. Peter D is not the father of the older children but has two female children from a previous long-term relationship aged 10 and 13, who he occasionally sees. Peter's relationship with his ex-partner is difficult and she is unhappy that he maintains contact with the chil-dren. Susan and Peter have been together for the last four months.

One Monday morning Peter hurriedly drops both children at the children's centre, ensuring that they are admitted to the classroom before he leaves. He seems distracted and does not interact with staff. The children appear very subdued according to the nursery nurse and at about 9.30 a.m., after the children had been in the centre for about half an hour, some bruising was noticed on both Benjamin's and Sasha's hands.

There are a number of features arising at this early stage that invite further exploration. An initial question concerns the possible injuries and whether they were likely to have been accidentally or purposefully caused. In attempting to ascertain what may have happened it is important to refer to the local authority child protection guidelines which advise that it is important that 'The procedures must be followed when there is concern that a child under the age of eighteen years may have suffered or be at risk of suffering harm ... ' (*Manchester City Council Child Protection Guidelines* 2005).

The child protection procedures are largely based on the Children Act 1989 and 'harm' in the Act under Section 31 refers to ill-treatment or the impairment of health or development. Ill-treatment may also be referred to as child abuse, of which there are four broad categories 'recognized internationally: physical abuse, emotional abuse, sexual abuse and neglect' (Colton *et al.* 2001: 126). The Children Act 1989 also reflects the concern to support children through its ten principles which place the welfare of the child as paramount. The principles emphasize the importance of responding without delay and of courts not making an order in relation to a child unless it considers that to make an order would be better for the child than not doing so. The principles also emphasize that children are best brought up by their families and that it is the parents who have the primary responsibility for doing so. There is therefore an onus on practitioners to develop a partnership with the child, parents and any other relevant persons including carers, provided that this is consistent with the child's welfare. In addition, full consultations should take place regarding any decisions that might affect the child.

It seems clear from considering the above set of principles that a parent should not be excluded when concerns are raised by practioners. Rather, it is expected that efforts will be made to develop a relationship that will be more like teamwork if the child's best interests are likely to be met. The principles also relate to the UN Convention on the Rights of the Child (in Powell 2001: 54) through Principles 2, 6 and 9 which refer to rights to 'protection by law, development, and ... the paramountcy of the child's best interests'; 'family support' and 'protection from neglect, cruelty and exploitation'.

These principles resonate with the *Birth to Three Matters* framework which recognizes four main themes that help in understanding young children and babies: a Strong Child, a Skilful Communicator, a Competent Learner and a

Healthy Child. As the literature review for the *Birth to Three Matters* framework suggests (David *et al.* 2003), in developing a Strong Child there is the need to relate to children as significant others with sensitivity and responsiveness. It may therefore be possible for the early years practitioner to engage any child for whom concern is felt as an individual and recognize her or him as having a developing sense of self and therefore as someone who may be able to articulate their experiences.

In the case study, after the practitioner recognized the bruises the children can be engaged with and their sense of self as 'strong' children and 'skilful communicators' can be appealed to. The framework points out that children are able to develop a voice which can be accessed and may lead to further understanding of their experiences. It is therefore sensible for any child presenting with a worrying mark or bruise to be asked for their version of what has happened. It is of course important for any questions to be asked with sensitivity and thoughtfulness as a means of supporting the child (this is emphasized in Finding a Voice in the *Birth to Three Matters* framework cards). In the situation outlined in the case study it is important to emphasize that having recognized the injury and spoken to the children the practitioner is referring to the first point of guidance concerning anyone who has a worry about a child who may be being abused (DfES 2005). This is reinforced through local child protection guidelines such as those available for practitioners (DfES 2005) which suggest the following.

Before making the referral

If there is a physical injury:

- ask the child and parent how it happened, make a note on the skin map if appropriate;
- consider the need for urgent treatment;
- make a note of what the child says;
- do not over-question or ask leading questions.

This should help the practitioner in forming a judgement about whether or not to refer to the local children and families department, while keeping the guidance referred to earlier at the forefront of their thinking.

The relationship between parents and childcare services

The nature of involvement that may develop between parents and childcare agencies can vary enormously, but for most of the time relations will tend to be mutually supportive and beneficial. However, when a situation as described in the case study arises it may be that the parents initially experience a range of emotions including anger and distrust, which in turn may lead to an initial breakdown in the relationship that exists between the family and the children's centre. Although it may be difficult at the time, it is probably helpful for a practitioner to remind parents that the children's centre has, like all other agencies that are involved with young children and their parents, a set of agreed child protection procedures which must be followed. From the parent's point of view it may well seem that they are being perceived as failures in the eyes of the practitioners who have raised concerns.

Guidelines also indicate that the practitioner should: 'Where possible, and provided that this will not place the child at greater risk of harm, discuss ... concerns with the family and seek their agreement before making the referral to Children, Families and Social Care' (*Manchester City Council Child Protection Guidelines* 2005). Childcare practitioners have a duty to recognize and then refer their concerns to the appropriate line manager or external agency. In the case of schools and Sure Start centres this would be the designated child protection coordinator who may then make a further referral to social workers at the children, families and social care department. It may be a difficult judgement for a practitioner to make to determine the level of risk to the child's well-being in their own family and it is probably important for a discussion to be initiated with the social worker in order to decide whether a referral at this stage is appropriate.

The parents' position

From the point of view of the parents the process of being on the receiving end of suspicion and an investigation into possible child abuse can be threatening, frightening and disempowering. It is significant therefore that practitioners are expected to work closely with parents at such a difficult time and jointly consider the child's well-being as a set of shared concerns. How willing will any parent be in participating in such a process particularly when the parents may be considered as the likely perpetrators of ill-treatment? The likely impact of any investigation may be to place the parents under a form of surveillance from a range of practitioners, family members and possibly community members. In terms of the case study Susan as the children's mother may reflect on the impact that the investigation is having on her family. For instance, does her relationship with Peter enter a difficult period? She may now distrust him and is likely to also experience guilty feelings arising from the possibility that she may be living with someone who she has introduced into the home with the potential and opportunity to harm her children. She may also be anxious that the children's birth father or other members of her wider family may hear of the concerns being expressed and attempt to confront her and Peter. The birth father (should he hear of what's happened) may also urge her to let the children be accepted into his care.

Of course these are only a few of a number of possible scenarios that may occur but it seems clear that the immediate impact of an investigation will tend to be negative rather than positive in the way that it is viewed by the parents and the family as a whole. In addition to an early response to family needs, there is substantial evidence that at-risk families have multiple and overlapping needs that cannot be met under one agency roof. Services need to be able to respond or know where families might gain assistance for their multiple needs (Durlak 1998). A comprehensive approach to family support also recognizes the impacts of family, cultural and social factors in children's development, and the relationship between intervening in these areas and subsequent improvements in child welfare (Bronfenbrenner 1979).

Thoburn *et al.* (1995) outline a range of difficulties that parents may face in their dealings with a multi-agency investigation that include:

* uncertainty about their rights;
* uncertainty about the roles of different agencies;
* difficulty about putting their views forward at case conferences;
* uncertainty that they are being listened to;
* uncertainty about what some of the procedural details such as registration mean.

The research concluded that 'the clearest message expressed by parents was the advantage of being there the whole time. When they were not they all wished that they could have been' (Thoburn *et al.* 1995: 8).

While it seems clear that comprehensive models of service delivery can provide the most effective interventions for children (O'Looney 1994; Ramey and Ramey 1998 cited in Wise 2003: 184), parents can and often do feel isolated by child protection processes. This is problematic since their involvement is central if the principles of partnership as expressed in the Children Act 1989 are to be met.

The picture as set out above suggests why parents might be deterred from cooperating with a child protection investigation. The child protection investigation process, in its attempt to protect the child, appears to risk alienating parents and the wider family since parents may feel that they are being viewed with some suspicion or alternatively that they are being judged as 'poor' parents. This sense of deficit can undermine opportunities for working together which require a more shared sense of power than an investigation can initially offer. There are clear issues concerning power and attempts to maintain positive working relationships in the early stages of an investigation. Petrie and Corby (2002: 388) indicate that in child protection ... 'The primary client is the child and there may be quite conflicting perspectives between the family adults and the professional workers as to the issues of risk and care'. In such situations there may already be difficulties concerning trust which, coupled with the legal and administrative powers available to social workers during an investigation, are likely in many cases to drive a wedge between parents and the practitioners rather than encourage partnership. The Children Act 1989 offers a framework for partnership arrangements and the message of working alongside parents is again emphasized in the Children Act 2004: 'The Act specifically requires authorities to have regard to the importance of parents and other persons caring for children when making arrangements under section 10' (www.everychildmatters.gov.uk).

Parents' sense of importance will tend to be tinged by the accompanying belief that practitioners may consider them to be not coping particularly well. The *Framework for the Assessment of Children in Need and their Families* (DoH 2000) suggests a scale of events that can 'make life difficult'. These offer a ranking procedure for each of the events to be considered during the process of assessment and include such everyday types of situation as: continually cleaning up mess; being nagged, whined at and complained to; and difficult mealtimes. These allow problems and difficult times to be identified and strategies to be developed to ease stressful aspects of the parent-child relationship. This is both helpful and supportive to parents as it acknowledges that there are pressures that contribute to moments of difficulty in childcare and may lead to inappropriate reactions and behaviour. Empathy is an important skill for practitioners to develop and employ at such fraught times as it helps them to reflect on the circumstances of the parents as well as the child. The interpersonal skills of the practitioners involved at each stage and their capacity to relate to the concerns of parents are an important element in developing a parent partnership scheme.

Many parent partnership schemes have been successfully set up, often in the voluntary sector, with the purpose of encouraging inclusion and a voice for parents (Lazarus 2000). However, the cumulative effect of these rather formal approaches is likely to highlight the sense that there is something 'lacking' in those parents who become involved unless part of the process is to identify strengths also.

The possibility for more positive shared work with parents presents itself through the developing Sure Start centres with their emphasis on offering a resource for the neighbourhood community and practitioners to use. A good example of the development of a local service operating from a children's centre is where the health visiting service set up a feeding group to deal with parental concerns about feeding difficulties being experienced by their children (Powell 2005). In the past, parents might have been referred by a health practitioner directly to a social worker if there were concerns that they were unable to cope with their child's needs and this might have resulted in the child becoming the focus of care proceedings. While such an option is still available and may be initiated in extreme cases, the feeding group offers an alternative option that is less interventionist and formal, making it more likely that parents will feel that they are involved as partners in the rearing process. Of course the feeding group may initially promote feelings of anxiety, especially as a number of practitioners including special care health visitors, paediatricians and social workers may be initially involved. However, this tends to reduce once the parents meet in the group context. It is there, in the group, that they are able to appreciate that other parents have similar issues about feeding which makes sharing less traumatic and the process of overcoming their child's feeding difficulties more likely to be successful. This process is far less stigmatizing and allows mealtimes to become a sociable and enjoyable experience with the opportunity for parents to play with their children and accept that mealtimes are often messy, tactile experiences. Parents are also encouraged to develop their attachments to their children through pleasurable experiences such as baby massage, singing together and eating lunch together (Beswick and Pendrill 2004: 15).

The development of the *Every Child Matters* framework emphasizes the importance of the involvement of parents in the life of Sure Start children's centres, where they have the opportunity to develop strong links and positive relationships in the community. There are other additional benefits which include the possibility of parents becoming involved in using the centre to develop their own learning. Walker *et al.* (2000) point out that:

> meeting the needs of parents and families were crucial elements of this initiative, all of which would be achieved through partnership working and the provision of health and human services through school sites. Schools were thus conceptualised as having the potential to become 'lifelong learning centres' and focal points of their communities'.
>
> (in Wilkin *et al.* (2003: 27)).

Extended schools have a great deal in common with Sure Start children's centres as both aim to develop a strong community presence and promote the inclusion of community members in partnership with practitioners.

The *Next Steps* and *Birth to Three Matters*

This chapter began with a reminder of the important part that parents play in the lives of their children. The discussion revealed that the implementation of child protection procedures can drive a wedge between parents, their wider family and the practitioners who are urged through current childcare legislation to work in partnership with them.

There are clearly strong links and resonances between *Every Child Matters: The Next Steps* (DfES 2004a) and the *Birth to Three Matters* document. Both approaches support the importance of the parents as generally the most appropriate people to be raising children. In *Every Child Matters* the central driving policy is that of inclusion and in that respect Sure Start children's centres and extended schools are seen as community resources that offer access to a range of childcare and parent support services. This approach aims to meet the needs of parents who are often isolated or marginalized and to include them within the daily life of the community. Clearly there are likely to be difficulties in reaching out to everyone but it is vital to reach parents who in child protection terms need to be supported in raising their children. *Every Child Matters: Change for Children* (DfES 2004b: 19) offers a thoughtful example from practice of the use of the common assessment framework in forming 'a team around the child' resulting in a period of direct work with a range of professional practitioners who are able to make and speed up existing referrals addressing the behaviour of the child: 'Due to this integrated approach to identifying the causes of M's behaviour, M's family now feel they are receiving coordinated support to meet his needs' (DfES 2004b:19).

The *Birth to Three Matters* emphasis on a child as Strong, a Skilful Communicator, a Competent Learner and a Healthy Child supports the view that children should be understood as holistic and competent beings, making clear connections to the aims of *Every Child Matters*. As Naomi Eisenstadt (2005: xv) the director of Sure Start points out:

> *Every Child Matters* emphasised the issues that consistently have been part of the early years approach: working with the whole child; bringing together concern for educational, social and health outcomes; working with parents as well as children. All these are well reflected in both the Foundation Stage and the Birth to Three Framework.

It is important to recognize when working with parents in the context of child protection that the support for their children may be extended to them as the child's most significant adult(s) who on occasion may need support to deal with difficulties before they deteriorate and require serious intervention from practitioners.

References

Beswick, J. and Pendrill, J. (2004) *The 'Feeding Service' Annual Report* (unpublished).

Bronfenbrenner, U. (1979) *The Ecology of Human Development Experiments by Nature and Design*. Cambridge, MA: Harvard University Press.

Colton, M., Sanders, R. and Williams, M. (2001) *An Introduction to Working with Children: A Guide for Social Workers*. Houndsmill: Palgrave.

David, T., Goouch, K., Powell, S. and Abbott, L. (2003) *Birth to Three Matters: A Review of the Literature*. London: DfES Publications.

DfES (2002) *Birth to Three Matters*. London: DfES Publications.

DfES (2004a) *Every Child Matters: The Next Steps*. London: DfES Publications.

DfES (2004b) *Every Child Matters: Change for Children*. London: DfES Publications.

DfES (2005) What to do if you're worried a child is being abused; Nottingham. DfES publications.

DoH (2000) *Framework for the Assessment of Children in Need and their Families*. London: TSO.

Durlak, J. (1998) Common risk factors and protective factors in successful intervention programs, *American Journal of Orthopsychiatry*, 68(4): 512–20.

Eisenstadt, N. (2005) Foreword, in L. Abbott and A. Langston (eds) *Birth to Three Matters: Supporting the Framework of Effective Practice*. Maidenhead: Open University Press.

HM Treasury (2003) *Every Child Matters*. London: TSO.

Lazarus, C. (2000) *Models of Good Practice and Parent Partnership – The Eastern Region*, presented at ISEC 2000.

Manchester City Council Child Protection Guidelines (2005) www.manchester.gov.uk.

O'Looney, J. (1994) Modelling collaboration and social services integration: a single state's experience with developmental and non-developmental models, *Administration in Social Work*, 18(1): 61–86.

Petrie, S. and Corby, B. (2002) Partnership with parents, in K. Wilson and A. James (eds) *The Child Protection Handbook*, 2nd edn. Edinburgh: Bailliere Tindal.

Powell, J. (2005) Safety matters, in L. Abbott and A. Langston (eds) *Birth to Three Matters: Supporting the Framework of Effective Practice*. Maidenhead: Open University Press.

Powell, R. (2001) *Child Law: A Guide For Courts and Practitioners*. Winchester: Waterside Press.

Ramey, C. and Ramey, S. (1998) Early intervention and early experience, *American Psychologist*, 53(2): 109–20.

Thoburn, J., Lewis, A. and Hemmings, D. (1995) *Paternalism or Partnership? Family Involvement in the Child Protection Process*. London: TSO.

Walker, K.E., Grossman, J.B. and Raley, R. with Fellerath, V. and Holton, G.I. (2000) *Extended Service Schools: Putting Programming in Place*, cited in A. Wilkin, R. White and K. Kinder (2003) *Towards Extended Schools: A Literature Review*, NFER Research Report 432. London: DfES Publications.

Wise, S. (2003) The child in family services: expanding child abuse prevention, *Australian Social Work*, 56(3): 183–96.

7 Evaluating Better Beginnings

Mary Rohl and Caroline Barratt-Pugh

In this chapter we describe how Better Beginnings, a library-initiated early literacy intervention programme that targets the parents of children under 3, was designed, implemented and evaluated in two communities in Western Australia. This literacy programme recognizes the central role of parents and primary carers in the development of young children. It is designed to build on parents' existing knowledge and children's experiences in the home to encourage and support the vital role of parents as their child's first teachers. The programme encourages parents to share books, rhymes and songs at home with their young children. It also encourages them to take out library membership for themselves and their babies and to take part in library-based activities. The programme is broadly based on the UK Bookstart programme (Wade and Moore 1993) and has been developed by Public Library Services at the State Library of Western Australia. The underlying aims of the programme relate to the four aspects of the young child identified in the *Birth to Three Matters* framework (DfES 2002). Encouraging parents to share books, songs and rhymes specifically supports the development of a Skilful Communicator and a Competent Learner and some aspects of a Strong Child.

Background to Better Beginnings

The purpose of Better Beginnings is to provide positive language and literacy influences for children in their first three years of life through parent-child interactions. Research suggests that children's home environments have a crucial effect on early literacy learning and that they learn their family's and community's literacy practices and the value placed on literacy through the process of socialization (Moll *et al.* 1992; Moll 1994; Gee 1996; Luke *et al.* 1996; Snow *et al.* 1998).

The main participants of the Better Beginnings programme are the parents of young children, which highlights the power of parental 'transfer of behaviour, beliefs, practices, expectations and potential to their progeny' (Gadsden 2000: 873). The programme encourages an ongoing exchange of information between early childhood professionals and families. It is related to a Western Australian government early years strategy that aims to improve the well-being of young children aged 0–8 years and is based on strong cooperation between state and local government service agencies and non-government service providers. In planning and developing the Better Beginnings programme, there has been a high degree of inter-agency cooperation and consultation, and engagement with local communities.

The importance of sharing books, songs and rhymes in the development of Skilful Communicators

The *Birth to Three Matters* framework recognizes the importance of sharing rhymes, songs, poems and stories with young children from an early age in that these activities provide opportunities for babies and children to listen to and focus on the language of others.

The four components that make up a Skilful Communicator are 'being together', 'finding a voice', 'listening and responding', and 'making meaning'. Being together involves the development of social relations and communication in warm and supportive relationships. In such relationships young children begin to find a voice as they make contributions to language and literacy interactions through sounds and first words. Listening and responding are important elements of becoming a Skilful Communicator when children are supported in the development of more complex ways of interacting. As children strive to make sense of their worlds through a variety of interactions they have increased access to more sophisticated ways of making meaning.

Since Better Beginnings recognizes that children's language and literacy development begins from birth, parents are invited to join the programme within the first weeks of their child's life. Information included in a resource pack given to parents at this time emphasizes the social, emotional and cognitive benefits of sharing books, songs and rhymes with very young babies. Being together with a key person in a close, warm and loving relationship allows the child to be acknowledged and affirmed through mutual enjoyment of book and song interactions. In such interactions babies begin to imitate sounds, recognize familiar voices and experience conversations concerning simple books (Neuman and Celano 2001a). Babies begin to find a voice as the adult focuses their attention on the book, accepting and building on their responses. In the earliest stages the adult will focus on labelling simple pictures and reinforcing any attempts to communicate as babies distinguish sound patterns and attempt to say words. In this way babies are encouraged to listen, respond and make meaning.

The importance of sharing books, songs and rhymes in the development of Competent Learners

The components that make up a Competent Learner in the *Birth to Three Matters* framework are 'making connections', 'being imaginative', 'being creative' and 'representing'. Babies are learners from birth as they explore the world, making connections through their senses between themselves and what is around them. They become increasingly imaginative and creative as they engage in a range of experiences that include experiencing the world through songs, rhymes and books and participating in related activities. Engagement in these experiences provides young children with representations of their realities and empowers them to begin using their own forms of representation, such as cooing, babbling, talking, singing, dancing, drawing and early attempts at writing.

In Better Beginnings, babies are helped to become Competent Learners within a family and community context. Early intervention at key transition points in children's lives (e.g. the first few months of life) has been identified as a key factor in successful outcomes of intervention programmes (Rodgers *et al.* 2004). Family literacy programmes that begin at the birth of a child and change through the infant and toddler years have the potential to lead to positive language and literacy outcomes for children. Supporting literacy learning from birth, within the family, helps children become competent learners. As they take part in interactions concerning books they can be helped to make connections between the content of books and their own lives. Books, songs and rhymes, as representations of children's worlds, can all stimulate imagination and creativity as young children explore and discover new knowledge.

In terms of the ongoing development of competent learners, much research shows that shared experiences with books (Wells 1985; Sulzby 1994; Bus *et al.* 1995; Neuman and Celano 2001b), rhymes and language play (Bradley and Bryant 1985) in the earliest years have the potential to bring about improved language and literacy outcomes for children. There is evidence that children learn new vocabulary from hearing books read aloud (Dickinson and Smith 1994). This is important for early literacy as it has been found that exposure to rich vocabulary and stimulating discussion in the years before formal school predicts later literacy development (Dickinson and Tabors 2002). Further, while a rich vocabulary may be achieved through discussion of everyday experiences, exposure to the rich and complex language of books may promote the more complex language associated with school (Frijters *et al.* 2000).

While we have seen that early experiences with books, songs and rhymes are important for later literacy development, some research has shown that interaction patterns in relation to book-sharing differ within and across cultures and socioeconomic groups (Bus *et al.* 2002). There is evidence that assisting parents from low socioeconomic backgrounds to identify with the importance of literacy practices that are similar to school literacy practices appears to lead to increased frequency of these practices (Wade and Moore 1996; Jay and Rohl 2005). Further, evidence from evaluation of family literacy programmes suggests that parents who are not used to sharing books may need ongoing support in selecting appropriate books and in scaffolding interaction (Bus *et al.* 1995; Neuman 1996). The Better Beginnings programme offers a range of opportunities for parents to build on and extend their existing literacy practices through parent workshops, storytime sessions, community resource kits and family reading centres. Evidence from research undertaken in the USA and the UK has shown that public library-based family literacy intervention programmes can result in significantly improved literacy outcomes for parents, children and other community members (Monsour and Carole 1993; Laughlin 2003; Collins *et al.* 2005).

The Better Beginnings programme

We have shown how sharing songs, rhymes and books within the family can help to contribute towards the development of skilful communicators and competent learners. We have also seen how Better Beginnings addresses these aspects of development in children aged from birth to 3. In the following sections we describe the components of the programme, its implementation, the role of professionals and some findings about its impact. The programme was designed and coordinated by state library personnel and includes the following resources:

- a resource pack (given to the parents of young babies shortly after their birth), containing a quality children's book, a colourful growth measurement chart with nursery rhymes printed on it and information about the value of reading to children, some titles of popular children's books and information about local library resources;
- library-based parent/child storytime sessions and workshops, involving young children and their parents and featuring public library, healthcare and other child development professionals;
- a training manual for healthcare professionals and community workers that provides them with information on the value of reading to young children and the resources and support available through the state-wide public library system;
- 'tool boxes' that promote resources for children and their families

and can be used in community centres, childcare centres, playgroups and hospitals as well as in high-traffic areas, such as shopping centres;
- family reading centres in libraries that provide interactive early childhood learning spaces;
- A website that promotes family literacy (www.liswa.wa.gov.au).

In the first year Better Beginnings was piloted in ten communities across Western Australia. It was evaluated by a group of university-based researchers (Barratt-Pugh *et al.* 2005). This evaluation focused on two of these communities, one of which was an outer metropolitan suburb that we called 'Sherwood'. Sherwood contained a range of residential settings and had a very small indigenous population. The other community, that we called 'Bura', was a remote mining town some 600 kilometres distant from the nearest major city with a somewhat larger indigenous population.

The evaluation of Better Beginnings included identification of key factors in its implementation from the perspectives of the parents and the professionals involved, evaluation of its effectiveness from the participants' perspectives, and factors that seemed to add to or detract from its effectiveness. Parent participants filled out two surveys, one soon after they had received the resource pack and one around six months later, that asked about home literacy practices including introducing babies to songs, rhymes and books. Parents were also asked about library membership and use, their reactions to the resource pack and their perceptions of library-based activities. After the second survey some of these parents (all mothers) were interviewed in their homes and some of their book-reading practices with their children were observed.

The first contact that parents had with Better Beginnings was the distribution of the resource pack to new mothers. It had been planned that it would be given to the mothers by the community health nurse at the child health clinic when they took their babies for the eight-week baby check-up. In the Sherwood community the mothers received their pack at this time from the nurse. However, in the Bura community it was seen as more appropriate for the local librarian to visit new mothers in the maternity hospital shortly after they had given birth. In both communities when the mothers were presented with the resource pack they were also given information about sharing books, songs and rhymes with babies, in addition to information about joining the library for themselves and their babies.

A particular feature of the implementation in the Bura community was that the local librarian made follow-up home visits to the new mothers who took part in the programme, brought them a variety of library resources and invited them to library activities. Sherwood mothers were invited to library activities at mothers' groups set up by the community health nurse and received follow-up phone calls from the local librarian.

We now turn to some of our findings about the programme in the two selected communities. In order to personalize these we tell part of the story from the perspective of Paula, a young mother from Sherwood. Paula was presented with the resource pack by the community health nurse when Tahlia, her first child, was eight weeks old and she was interviewed for the project seven months later. Before leaving work for Tahlia's birth Paula had worked in a childcare centre. She had a TAFE (technical college) qualification in the area; her partner Pete had left school at 15 years of age. Paula indicated that there were fewer than 50 books in the home; she and her partner read cookery books, gardening books, magazines and junk mail which they sometimes shared with Tahlia.

Changes in parent perceptions and behaviours following involvement in Better Beginnings

As the programme was initiated and coordinated by the state library, it was important that we collected information about library-related behaviours and perceptions as well as home literacy. After being involved in Better Beginnings for about six months, half of the mothers who had not previously been library members had joined the library. Further, a majority reported that Better Beginnings had changed their opinion that babies could have library membership and a third had indeed taken out library membership for their babies. Most of those with library memberships borrowed books for themselves and their babies and half of these mothers also borrowed videos, CDs and DVDs for their babies. Paula, who already had library membership for herself before Tahlia's birth, had taken out library membership for her baby on the basis of information received in the Better Beginnings resource pack. She made monthly visits to the library when she borrowed books for her baby and had taken part in some library baby storytime sessions. She explains:

> She [the librarian] explained how to read and how to do different things as well. The other mums at my playgroup that went were just amazed at all the different things you can do with stories, you know like finger puppets and bits and pieces like that to bring stories to life, which I mean I'd seen everything before being in childcare but they were all just going, 'Wow, this is really great!'

Parents who took part in Better Beginnings also reported various changes in their opinions and practices in terms of sharing books, songs and rhymes with their babies and in their library use as a result of their involvement in the programme. At the time of the second survey all but one of the mothers indicated that they shared rhymes and songs with their babies. As Paula put it, 'I sing to her all the time, so she's used to it ... she's got a couple of favourites that she loves'.

At this time almost all reported sharing books with their babies and many reported that they had changed their opinions about the value of this practice. Paula reported that the programme had definitely changed her opinions and practices with regard to reading to babies, despite the fact that she had previously worked with babies and toddlers in the childcare context:

> I didn't even think about, you know, reading to them from birth ... like even when they're still in the stomach! Yes, I mean, I've worked in a baby's room in daycare and we read books but we sort of read them to the toddlers and the babies just sort of watched, so it wasn't really aimed at the babies. But, yes, I've been reading books ... and just showing her things and she loves it! Most of the time she's already keeping them up the right way. She knows how to turn pages. She'll sit by herself. I've just a couple of weeks ago bought her little books like this, at her level, so she can get to them when she wants and she'll go and pull them down and turn the pages and look through them.

In addition to Tahlia's obvious enjoyment of books, Paula identified other benefits related to sharing books with her baby. She thought that reading to Tahlia was accelerating the child's speech development and enhancing her ability to concentrate. With reference to emotional benefits, Paula said that books tended to 'calm' Tahlia and strengthened their relationship.

When reading to their babies, the mothers who were interviewed were observed to be following many of the strategies recommended in the Better Beginnings resources. Such strategies can be seen in Paula's report of her practices in reading to Tahlia. When Paula read to Tahlia, she would usually sit her on her lap and read the book before relating it to the child's world. Sometimes she would read the book twice in a single sitting. Tahlia had several favourite books that were read repeatedly from day to day:

> We probably read it a couple of days in a row and she usually grabs the same one at this age, now. When she was younger I'd read it a couple of times one after the other because once is not enough. Now that she's older as well, like, I was reading it in reference to other things, like we've got one book, I think, its friends or things that we do – so we've got toys on one page, faces on another and that and she loves that! And I'll pull faces like the pictures and stuff like that. The other book is colours, so we've sat there and looked. OK, that's the red page and all these red things and I'll point the red things out in the room ...

Paula was observed reading to Tahlia with great expression and ex-aggerated intonation. In the following excerpt from a transcript of her reading aloud to her baby Paula pointed at objects in the pictures, named them, described their attributes and purposes and asked questions as Tahlia responded by pointing, babbling, smiling, touching the book and turning the pages:

> And it's got the same pages that are in your other book too. I can count bricks in the trolley, one, two, three! Where are the bricks? Look, the three bricks to make a tower! One, two, three! The ball is very bouncy. It's time to play on my bike. What game shall I play? Look! Here's a car, brmm, brmm, I've got a big blue car. There's my ducks. This toy makes lots of noises. Here's the drum, bang, bang, bang, bang, bang, rattle and shake. This is fun. Oh a rattle! Do you want to look at it?

Paula or Pete would read to Tahlia daily in a fairly stable routine. Paula read to her once in the morning and once in the afternoon; Pete read the bedtime story.

The parents' views of programme implementation

In their survey responses the mothers were overwhelmingly positive about the resource pack as a whole, with almost all finding the book to be useful or very useful. Paula explained that she had received two Better Beginnings books and that these had become Tahlia's favourites. Most mothers had appreciated the nursery rhyme growth chart, but a few had asked for some modifications. Paula explained that she had put it on the wall and used it for reading the rhymes and drawing Tahlia's attention to the pictures. Most mothers did not want anything else added to the pack but a few asked for modifications that concerned durability of the materials, particularly the nursery rhyme growth chart, or additional information on literacy development. The pamphlets provided with the pack did not appear to be useful to some parents as they could not recall receiving them among all the information that they had been given by health and allied professionals at the time of the birth of their babies. Paula, while she did not remember being given an information leaflet, recalled the community health nurse 'going through' one with her. Paula also could not clearly remember the book list, but she had been given information about children's books by the librarian at the library baby storytime sessions.

In terms of implementation of the programme by the professionals involved, most of the mothers who were interviewed felt that the resource pack had been well explained to them. Paula felt that the presentation of the pack by the community health nurse was particularly helpful as she had presented the information twice, once at the eight-week check-up and again at a mothers' group meeting:

> She explained it when she gave it to us and explained the importance of, you know, reading from basically day one. You know by the time they're 12 months they can hold it up the right way, turn the pages, do all that! And we went through it again at a mothers' group a few weeks later when all the other mothers were there too, the young mothers in the area, and she spoke about it.

At the time of our evaluation of Better Beginnings the library-based activities were in the early stages of development and not all mothers had been made aware of them. Nevertheless, a third of mothers had taken part in the baby storytime sessions and a few fathers as well as mothers had attended parent-child workshops at the library. On the whole these parents found the activities to be very useful and some suggested modifications for future sessions. Paula had attended both types of activity. While she had enjoyed the first two baby storytime sessions that were limited to babies only, the third session had included older children and she felt that another session should be provided for older siblings whose behaviour she had found to be distracting. Paula had found the parent workshop sessions very useful, especially as the librarian had given information packs to the parents on topics such as rhymes for them to say when bouncing children on their knees.

What seemed to facilitate the implementation?

The appointment of a state library-based programme coordinator with responsibility for the design, training and implementation of the programme meant that it was coordinated consistently across the communities. She managed the collaboration between partner agencies at a central and community level, thus ensuring that the programme was inclusive in terms of the professionals involved. This collaboration, particularly in the development and distribution of the resource pack, ensured that stakeholders' voices were heard and that modifications could be made quickly where indicated. Further, because she had an overview of the whole project the coordinator was able to ensure that the programme was flexible in terms of meeting the needs of different communities.

The commitment, enthusiasm and shared goals of the community health nurses and librarians helped them work collaboratively towards the aims of Better Beginnings. Collaboration between these professionals at state and local levels was crucial for the effective distribution of the resource packs and information about health and library resources. The community health nurses felt that the programme complemented their work with families and familiarity with the training materials helped them to communicate more effectively the value of sharing books, songs and rhymes with babies. They were also able to talk to new mothers about joining and using the library, reassuring them that children of all ages were welcome.

Flexibility of the programme implementation in the two communities allowed it to be delivered in ways that were appropriate for each. In Sherwood the resource pack was given to new mothers at the child health clinic, whereas in Bura the librarian delivered the pack to the mothers in hospital. This flexibility enabled the programme to be extended through a range of community groups. For example, in Bura the librarian joined an indigenous playgroup held outdoors in a local park, where she read and told stories. It also fostered sharing of professional expertise as librarians gave talks at mothers' groups organized by healthcare workers, and speech pathologists were invited to talk to parents at library workshops.

What were the issues identified in the implementation?

While we have seen that the implementation of Better Beginnings was highly successful in that it resulted in various positive outcomes, a number of issues for consideration were identified. Establishing partnerships between agencies was identified as an initial challenge as it was at times difficult to identify the person within an agency who had the authority to make a commitment to the programme.

Another important issue of concern was the extra work that Better Beginnings entailed for the community health nurses and librarians in that these enthusiastic and passionate people were involved in developing and implementing activities for which they were given no additional time allowance. Further, some of the librarians and community health nurses indicated that they had received little initial professional training in early years literacy learning. While they had acquired new learning and skills during the course of the programme through the training pack they still saw a need for targeted professional development in this area.

Given the diverse nature of the Australian population (one in four children live in a household where a language other than English is spoken), the limited availability of suitable books and other materials depicting a variety of cultural, ethnic and family groups was identified as an issue of inclusivity. This has been addressed in modifications made to some elements of the pack. During the course of the programme some communities created and published their own board books. In addition, the state library consulted with publishers in order to commission more appropriate resources. Another issue of inclusivity was the presentation of information in brochure format that was not appropriate for some parents with low literacy skills. This has been addressed in that the brochures have been replaced by large colourful posters that depict literacy practices in a range of Australian families and contain information in a simplified and more readable format. Nevertheless, the issue of how to engage non-traditional library users in the programme remains a challenge. A community health nurse remarked, 'We're not reaching the families who need Better Beginnings the most', and a librarian put it this way: 'I think as a library we're not going to make any progress until we've got an indigenous person working on the staff that can go out and do the home visits and can encourage Aboriginal families to come in and use the library'.

Sustainability of the programme was identified as an issue of concern. On the whole the library-based activities were not well attended. These were an important element of the programme in that they were planned to sustain and extend parent understanding and skills in sharing books, songs and rhymes with their babies and young children. It appeared that problems of communication and timing could have compromised attendance at these events. For example, some parents had not received information about the activities, while others felt that sessions held in the evening were too difficult for parents of young children to attend. Nevertheless, the evening sessions did attract some fathers, which was most important in terms of both inclusion and sustainability of the programme. Whilst the initial engagement of mothers in the programme during the first months of a child's life is important, it is even more important that family involvement is maintained over a substantial period of time.

Conclusions

In this chapter we have shown how Better Beginnings reflects a number of significant aspects of the philosophy and practices outlined in the *Birth to Three Matters* framework. Better Beginnings also has strong links to research from other family literacy programmes such as Bookstart in the UK, which show that intervention programmes can have positive outcomes for children's later literacy development (Wade and Moore 1996). In addition we have shown that the Better Beginnings has the potential to support parents in their role as their child's first teacher. As a result of this finding the programme is being delivered across Western Australia over a four-year period to a range of communities that represent diverse geographical, social, cultural and economic contexts. Our findings give rise to a number of questions that professionals working with parents of young children may like to consider. These address some of the issues that we identified in our evaluation of the programme and may be categorized in terms of the design and implementation of the programme itself and issues concerning professional roles.

Reflective questions about programme issues

- How may professionals setting up a programme for parents of young children ensure that the needs of a diverse range of communities can be met?
- How may professionals working with parents of young children establish and maintain partnerships with them that include parent involvement in programme development?
- Which factors need to be considered in the presentation of resources for parents in order to ensure inclusivity in terms of cultural and linguistic background and levels of literacy?
- How may families be reached who traditionally do not become involved in mainstream community activities?

Reflective questions about professional issues

- What are the qualities necessary for the role of coordinator of large multi-faceted projects?
- How may partnerships between professionals in programmes that involve inter-agency collaboration be established and maintained?
- How may professionals involved in new initiatives be supported in terms of professional development in specific areas?
- How may existing professional roles be redefined in order to incorporate time allowance for collaboration with other agencies and parents?

Acknowledgements

This research was funded through an Edith Cowan University Industry Collaboration Grant in collaboration with State Library of Western Australia. We would like to acknowledge Margaret Allen (CEO of the State Library of Western Australia) and Sue North (Better Beginnings programme coordinator) for their ongoing commitment to the evaluation of Better Beginnings. We would also like to acknowledge the important contribution made by Grace Oakley and Jessica Elderfield to the Better Beginnings research project, particularly in relation to data collection and analysis.

References

Barratt-Pugh, C., Rohl, M., Oakley, G. and Elderfield, J. (2005) *Better Beginnings: An Evaluation from Two Communities*, www.liswa.wa.gov.au.

Bradley, L. and Bryant, P.E. (1985) *Rhyme and Reason in Reading and Spelling*. Ann Arbor, MI: University of Michigan Press.

Bus, A.G., Van Ijzendoorn, M. H. and Pellegrini, A.D. (1995) Joint book reading makes for success in learning to read: a meta-analysis on intergenerational transmission of literacy, *Review of Educational Research*, 65: 1–21.

Bus, A.G., Leseman, P.P.M. and Keultjes, P. (2002) Joint book reading across cultures: a comparison of Surinamese-Dutch, Turkish-Dutch, and Dutch parent–child dyads, *Journal of Literacy Research*, 32: 53–76.

Collins. F., Svensson, C. and Mahony, H. (2005) *Bookstart: Planting a Seed for Life*. London: Booktrust.

DfES (2002) *Birth to Three Matters*. London: DfES Publications.

Dickinson, D.K. and Smith, M.W. (1994) Long-term effects of preschool teachers' book readings on low income children's vocabulary and story comprehension, *Reading Research Quarterly*, 29: 104–22.

Dickinson, D.K. and Tabors, P. (2002) Fostering language and literacy in classrooms and homes, *Young Children*, 57(2): 10–18.

Frijters, J.C., Baron, R.W. and Brunello, M. (2000) Direct and mediated influences of home literacy and literacy interest on prereaders' oral vocabulary and early written language skill, *Journal of Educational Psychology*, 92: 466–77.

Gadsden, V. L. (2000) Intergenerational literacy within families, in M.L. Kamil, P.B. Mosenthal, P.D. Pearson and R. Barr (eds) *Handbook of Reading Research*, vol. 3. Mahwah, NJ: Lawrence Erlbaum Associates.

Gee, J.P. (1996) Literacy and social minds, in G. Bull and M. Anstey (eds) *The Literacy Lexicon*. Sydney: Prentice Hall.

Jay, J. and Rohl, M. (2005) Constructing a family literacy program: challenges and successes, *International Journal of Early Childhood*, 37(1): 57–78.

Laughlin, S. (2003) *Public Library Association/Association of Library Service for Children Early Literacy Project: 2003 Evaluation*. Bloomington, IN: Public Library Association.

Luke, A., Comber, B. and O'Brien, J. (1996) Critical literacies and cultural studies, in G. Bull and M. Anstey (eds) *The Literacy Lexicon*. Sydney: Prentice Hall.

Moll, L.C. (1994) Literacy research in community and classrooms: a sociocultural approach, in B. Ruddell, M.R. Ruddell and H. Singer (eds) *Theoretical processes and Models of Reading*, 4th edn. Newark, DE: International Reading Association.

Moll, L., Amanti, C., Neff, D. and Gonzalez, N. (1992) Funds of knowledge for teaching: using a qualitative approach to connect homes and classrooms, *Theory into Practice*, 31(2): 132–41.

Monsour, M. and Carole, T. (1993) *Library-Based Family Literacy Projects*. Chicago, IL: American Library Association.

Neuman, S.B. (1996) Children engaging in storybook reading: the influence of access to print resources, opportunity and parental interaction, *Early Childhood Research Quarterly*, 11: 495–513.

Neuman, S.B. and Celano, D. (2001a) Books Aloud: a campaign to 'put books in children's hands', *The Reading Teacher*, 54: 550–7.

Neuman, S.B. and Celano, D. (2001b) Access to print in low-income and middle income communities, *Reading Research Quarterly*, 36: 8–26.

Rodgers, P., Edgecombe, G. and Kimberley, S. (2004) *Evaluation of the Stronger Families and Communities Strategy 2000-2004*. Canberra: DFCS.

Snow, C.E., Burns, M.S. and Griffin, P. (eds) (1998) *Preventing Reading Difficulties in Young Children*. Western Washington, DC: National Academy Press.

Sulzby, E. (1994) Children's emergent reading of favorite story books: a developmental study, in R.B. Ruddell and H. Singer (eds) *Theoretical Models and Processes of Reading*, 4th edn. Newark, DE: International Reading Association.

Wade, B. and Moore, M. (1993) *Bookstart*. London: Book Trust.

Wade, B. and Moore, M. (1996) Children's early book behaviour, *Educational Review*, 48(3): 283–9.

Wells, G. (1985) *The Meaning Makers*. Portsmouth, NH: Heinemann.

8 Health Matters

Elizabeth Howard

My present position is as a Health Lead for Sure Start, which is a government initiative focusing on support for families with children up to 4 years of age. My professional development has always involved work focused on the lives of families, babies and young children. Having had a background in nursing, both in hospital and the community, I then trained and worked as a health visitor. This really gave me a passion for child development as I was able to observe interactions between parents and their children. Prior to this period, I had worked directly with families in their own homes, but health visiting really concentrated my thoughts on the behaviour of children. Following this, I studied for a B.Sc. honours degree in psychology, focusing on observations of children and analysis of and reflection on their behaviour, while coming to a better understanding of parental attitudes to behaviour. A teaching qualification then led me to teach childcare in a college of further education. During this period, I was often frustrated by the system where I had to plead to teach child development as this was traditionally taught by teachers and was not really considered to be a topic which could be addressed by the health team, of which I was a member. There was, in these courses, often some difficulty in bringing all aspects of health together within a holistic viewpoint, since much of the body of knowledge was divided up for the purposes of teaching. Subsequently my career route took me away from teaching, back to direct work with families and it is in this context that I have come to be familiar with the *Birth to Three Matters* framework (DfES 2002), and where I have recognized its potential as a tool for learning and teaching for health professionals involved with families of young children.

My first introduction to the *Birth to Three Matters* framework happened when I viewed the video which is part of the package. I was greatly impressed by the holistic approach it took, and delighted at the very positive attitudes shown towards babies and young children by the carers. A colleague from early years then invited me to train as a trainer for *Birth to Three Matters* and I immediately felt that I would like to introduce this programme to the health visiting team to facilitate work with families in areas of deprivation and to have the opportunity to work with others and be involved in this and other new initiatives.

Health matters

This chapter will examine ways to support the health and well-being of young children with reference to the *Birth to Three Matters* framework, particularly the aspect of a Healthy Child, which brings together evidence about young children's mental and physical well-being. The reduction of socioeconomic inequalities, which have been shown to lead to differences in children's health, is a major concern of the Sure Start programme at both national and local level. The same factors have an influence on the number of accidents that happen to young children and also have an effect on nutrition. Wachs (2000) reviews the evidence from research into the links between nutritional deficits and behavioural development. He reports, among other findings, that poor nutrition can lead to problems such as general and specific cognitive deficits; lower neonatal reactivity; apathy; irritability; lower activity levels and higher inhibition; and increased risk of poorer cognitive and academic performance respectively. Clearly, such recent research adds to our knowledge of child development, and this should be reflected in our attitude towards children and the way we care for them.

It therefore seems important that health professionals are able to observe all four related aspects described in the *Birth to Three Matters* framework, but for the purposes of this chapter consideration will be given to the four components of the aspect of a Healthy Child, visually:

- emotional well-being;
- growing and developing;
- keeping safe;
- healthy choices.

Overall, there are many people in the health visiting team including, in addition to the health visitor, nursery nurses, staff nurses and health visitor assistants, who all work together to provide the best possible service to families. The administrative staff are also involved in the organization of the Sure Start programme through their work in providing information for the public, and monitoring the number and type of visits in the community.

The Sure Start programme has allowed these teams to provide opportunities to develop support groups and has provided places for parents and young children to meet, in a safe and well-managed environment, with professionals on hand to support them in parenting their children. It also encourages parents to become involved in decision-making and in working with children themselves. Help is also given to parents who wish to train for future employment. Clearly, while some of this work already existed there has nonetheless been a dramatic increase in this area recently, in line with government initiatives, and Sure Start has focused firmly on the early years as this has been shown to be a very important area for future development. Evaluation of every intervention takes place so that successful projects may then be mainstreamed and other participants may benefit from what has been learned in individual programmes.

This is consistent with Gerhardt's (2004) view that, prevention is better than cure. Indeed, as she argues, there is a growing recognition that finding ways to improve the relationship between parents and their babies is a much more cost-effective (and less painful) way of improving mental health than involvement in a growing number of adult therapeutic treatments. She also reminds us that there are insufficient mental health workers to work with parents and their babies and that often problems are not thought to be in need of treatment until the baby is older and is displaying obvious signs of distress. She suggests that health visitors could be involved in supporting families by offering expertise in this domain.

This knowledge led me to believe that training in the use of the *Birth to Three Matters* framework would be useful for all practitioners working in the health visitor team, to allow them to extend and build their own levels of knowledge and expertise about effective practice with babies and young children, and guide them to the underpinning research material in *Birth to Three Matters: A Review of the Literature* (David *et al.* 2003).

Interestingly, in reflecting on the composition of many health teams it seems that nursery nurses are likely to have had most training in childcare and child development, while health visitors are well-trained in all aspects of the health of the whole family. Similarly, many other workers who are involved with families from a health perspective, and will from time to time be involved in discussions about children's development, may have received training in a variety of issues such as behaviour management, but again may not have studied child development to any depth. This group includes family support workers, parent involvement workers and others. However, all could benefit from learning about the framework, particularly those professionals who trained before the publication of *Birth to Three Matters* in 2002.

Many Sure Start programmes have been developed and all work towards the Sure Start targets and take into consideration the needs of the area and the views of the parents, although there is much variation across the country depending upon the way partnerships have been developed and on the needs of local communities. Sure Start also provides opportunities to share successes at conferences or seminars. One programme will be briefly described here, remembering that in one Primary Care Trust (PCT) there may be a number of programmes with varied coordination, and sometimes sharing of funding. The programme with which I am most familiar, and which I will discuss, offers a variety of projects affecting parents. These include:

- A breastfeeding project, where workers within the trust, mainly health visitors, alongside other disciplines, train with the La Leche League and in turn train parents, grandparents and others, who have themselves breastfed their own babies. A group, known as Breast Mates, is formed, and its members then work in the community alongside professionals to support breastfeeding mothers and to promote the importance of breastfeeding.
- A speech and language project, in which a speech therapist and community development worker provide a service to families in the Sure Start programme. Professionals set up support groups, undertake home visits and offer early access to speech therapy for children whose parents have concerns about their children's speech and language development.
- A family support project which offers families support during times of need, for example regarding the birth of a new baby, bereavement or during stressful periods and illness.
- A parental involvement project involving a parental involvement worker which provides support to parents and encourages them to set up and run parent forums. It also gives support to those who wish to study, or find employment.
- A Book Start project which provides a Sure Start worker who, along with staff from library services, offers storytimes for children and organizes special outings and other activities to encourage babies and young children to develop a love of books and stories.
- A community play project, staffed by a community play worker, which offers 'Stay and Play' sessions and other outings and activities for parents and children to enjoy together.
- A baby care project, run by a midwife, which provides special visits and sessions for mothers, including a baby massage group.
- A nutrition project that includes weaning groups and 'Cook and Taste' sessions, based on healthy eating.
- A perinatal project that allows extra support to be given to parents suffering from depression. It helps prevent more long-term effects of depression by offering intervention in the form of early diagnosis and support.
- A domestic violence project which promotes the Freedom Programme, giving women the opportunity to attend groups, and provides workers from several disciplines to give help at a time of need.
- A safety project that provides safety equipment for families on low incomes, or in need. Safety visits are offered at home to provide advice and guidance on safety in the home, ironically the most dangerous place for young children.
- A Lifestart project that offers the Webster-Stratton (1999) parenting

programme, which helps parents who are having problems with managing their children's behaviour.

All of these programmes would seem to chime with the idea that parents need help at specific times in their lives, to facilitate the needs of their children, and that professionals need to have enough knowledge to enable them to work with parents and to provide effective support.

Emotional well-being

The health visiting team is essential to most Sure Start projects. They, along with the midwife, offer a visit to every family with a new baby and, by their attitude, can influence how parents act and feel towards their children. Parents sometimes find it hard to understand their children's emotions and may try to find a common-sense explanation for a particular behaviour, sometimes believing that the baby is intentionally demanding more attention than necessary, or that they are wilful in some way. Often there can be unrealistic expectations before a child is born, and where there are confusions about what is the expected behaviour of a newborn, or a 3-month-old baby, the health visitor can be very helpful in explaining to parents about child development. He or she might discuss the place of actions such as 'turn-taking' in language development and could help a new parent to have the confidence to know that comforting a child is not 'spoiling' them. I have found that parents often seem to know when their babies need comforting but are sometimes embarrassed or uncertain about doing this in the presence of others, 'especially' if they believe it is contrary to the expectations of the wider family. Health visitors can reaffirm that mothers and fathers are very important to the child and that everything they do with that child will contribute to the child's well-being.

Hall and Ellman (2003) suggest that insecure infant-parent attachment is an important predictor of social and emotional problems in later life, and may lead to similar problems in the next generation. Baby massage sessions, recommended in the *Birth to Three Matters* framework, support emotional development and help parents to spend special time being close to their children. This sets a pattern of touching which may last a lifetime. Many professionals know that if the mother is relaxed and content, the baby usually is also more relaxed. At around 6–9 months health visitors can help mothers understand why their babies cry on separation; this is another area where parents who are prepared for this stage will understand and manage the situation, so again the help of the health team can be invaluable.

'Stay and Play' sessions, as previously discussed, allow a child to explore and gain confidence with a known adult close by. I have observed a child entering the group as a baby and by the age of 13 months he is hurtling round the room pushing a trolley with pure glee on his face, his mother running round after him to make sure he is alright. With no playmates at home, one can only imagine his joy at the freedom in a large room with the security of his mother close by. In this case the nursery nurse had invited the mother and her baby to join the group; the play leader welcomed her and had provided suitable play facilities for the group. The play leader had a flexible attitude to the children and she seldom missed the chance to allow them to explore new things. Children wandered in and out of her singing and dance sessions as they pleased and learned to enjoy and anticipate the sessions. On one occasion one boy asked his grandma to switch on the music after the play worker had finished, and began to dance. Grandma called me in to watch as she knew I loved to see him dance, and before long other children joined in and they danced around the room in a line. This was a joy to see and demonstrated all the good things about Sure Start support – for example, confidence-building, approval, freedom, joy and also learning through play. Another time I watched a group of 3-year-old girls become friends, playing and chatting to each other, as their confidence and independence grew. Later I met the father of one of the girls who told me they had started nursery class together and how delighted he had been to see them all playing together in the playground, having settled in, after the huge transition from home to school.

Wonderful things happen in the community! Many times the play leader provides the opportunities, the nursery nurse points the way, the dental worker visits to provide advice and toothbrushes; outings are decided on with the parents and grandparents. Sometimes grandparents attend with children to allow a harassed mum to have some time to herself. Fruit is supplied mid-afternoon, while adult drinks are only allowed behind the safety gate, where children are not allowed, and so the adults often make friends. Problems are discussed and referrals made, and the speech and language community development worker becomes known to the parents so they can speak to them personally if they have concerns about their child's language development. Utopia! If only all children attended!

Health promotion has been described as that which is planned and informed, designed to improve physical or mental health and which prevents disease, disability or premature death (Hall and Ellman 2003). Furthermore, it is suggested that childhood health results from not only biological and genetic factors but also from environmental factors, including parent lifestyle and things such as housing and unemployment. Moylett and Djemli discuss how practitioners matter in supporting parents and how much 'parents look to practitioners to help them instigate change' (2005: 61). Making the *Birth to Three Matters* framework materials available to parents would seem to be a positive step forward in extending this support. Groups in which parents and children meet together with professionals offer ideal opportunities for helping parents to understand how the framework can be used to support them in their day-to-day lives with their children. Leaders of groups can study the material and work to further develop learning and to increase their own and parents' knowledge and understanding. Ideally, it would seem that prospective parents should also have every opportunity to discuss and learn more about the abilities of the newborn and about child development

Growing and developing

Surely the most difficult concept for both childcare professionals and parents is the conundrum that children grow and develop as a result of exploratory behaviour, which sometimes involves risk. Managing this risk always requires adults' presence, and sometimes requires their intervention yet, at the same time, it may require them to stand back, once they have ascertained that the child is safe. Bruce and Meggit confirm also that 'The most important factors for healthy development are that you should recognize the skills a child has developed and provide plenty of opportunities to practice them' (2003: 139). Growing and developing focuses on ways of supporting children as they gain control of their bodies, acquire physical skills and learn to be active. An important point to support this component that health workers can take into consideration while working with parents and children is encapsulated in the following quotation: 'Physical care and loving attention is required in different ways as a toddler becomes more mobile ... Exploratory behaviour ... takes the child away as she crawls, walks and inspects the world around her. The educator is required not only to protect the child through closeness, but also to let go to encourage growing autonomy' (Selleck and Griffin 1996: 157).

Another area which has become recognized as a contributing factor in healthy growth and development is nutrition, which has become a priority of government and health services. The health visiting team has always been influential in offering support to parents in relation to nutrition and now weaning groups are being developed in some areas, encouraging parents to provide fresh, as opposed to processed, food for their children. So, the role of health workers is highly significant in influencing parents to make healthy choices on their children's behalf.

Encouraging independence

I have often found parents to be confused and even aggrieved when their young children say 'no'; they may also find it difficult to comprehend their repeated use of the negative. Similarly, young children can be confused when their parents say 'no' to them. However, it is important that parents know how to encourage their children to be assertive and for them to be helped to recognize that what may appear to be unacceptable behaviour – refusing to comply with the parent's request – may in fact be behaviour to be positively encouraged since it relates to the way children can make their voices heard by adults. This is an opportunity for health professionals to share with parents how the *Birth to Three Matters* framework describes a healthy child, and can lead to a real understanding of the child as an emerging person, with their own thoughts, wishes and emotions.

One of the biggest problems for which parents seek help is the temper tantrum, and although there seems to be an improved understanding more recently, perhaps due to the proliferation of support groups, information and advice from the media, especially television and the internet, parents often feel that they are engaged in a battle of wills rather than experiencing the effects of a child's frustration. Knowledge can help both parent and child to be less stressed. Rodd (1996) suggests that sensitive early childhood professionals understand toddlers' needs for choice and decision-making opportunities. They understand that a 2-year-old might even say 'no' when they mean 'yes' and they are tolerant of toddlers' changes of mind. They provide opportunities for toddlers to cooperate by not demanding compliance but rather by offering simple alternatives as to how the needs of the situation might be met: 'If children do not feel that they are autonomous and independent beings, they may display developmentally immature and dependent behaviours and will find it difficult to display initiative later' (Rodd 1996: 22–3).

Healthy choices

In the review of literature which underpins the *Birth to Three Matters* framework, David *et al.* (2003) help us to understand that from birth young babies show preferences for people and for what they want to see, hear and taste and they continually discover more about what they like and dislike. As young children become more mobile and their boundaries widen, they make choices that involve real risk-taking, becoming more aware that choices have consequences. Opportunities for choices need to be provided and children's decisions valued. In this way parents begin to recognize what their children want.

Parents now have access to a great deal of information about childcare, and many possess excellent parenting skills. However, some do not, and most of us recognize that we did not know everything when our own children were young. Many different professionals are now involved in working with children and in supporting families. It is my belief that all professionals can benefit from studying the *Birth to Three Matters* materials in order to help and support parents and understand their difficulties. As a result of this, parents could have the opportunity to learn more about child development and the needs of children. Opportunities for discussion together with group support can help them in doing this.

Many children are now involved in out-of-home care, but they go home to their parents at the end of each day. Although different professionals help out or visit from time to time, children live with their parents, who are recognized as their child's first teachers, and the most important people in their lives. Some of the key messages that health workers can take to parents may be about understanding the importance of and meeting children's needs in relation to:

- attachment;
- separation anxiety;
- temper tantrums;
- feeding;
- opportunities for independence;
- praise and encouragement;
- feeling special.

If all parents had these understandings, it is likely that there would be less need for interventions from health professionals at a later stage, and the adage that prevention is better than cure would never be more true.

References

Abbott, L. and Langston, A. (2004) *Birth to Three Matters: Supporting the Framework of Effective Practice*. Maidenhead: Open University Press.

Bruce, T. and Meggitt, C. (2002) *Child Care and Education*, 3rd edn. London: Hodder & Stoughton.

David, T., Goouch, K., Powell, S. and Abbott, L. (2003) *Birth to Three Matters: A Review of the Literature*. London: DfES Publications.

DfES (2002) *Birth to Three Matters*. London: DfES Publications.

Gerhardt, S. (2004) *Why Love Matters*. London: Routledge.

Hall, D.M.B. and Elliman, D. (2003) *Health for all Children,* 4th edn. Oxford: Oxford University Press.

Moylett, H. and Djemli, P. (2005) Practitioners matter, in L. Abbott and A. Langston *Birth to Three Matters: Supporting the Framework of Effective Practice*. Maidenhead: Open University Press.

Rodd, J. (1996) *Understanding Young Children's Behaviour*. London: Allen & Unwin.

Selleck, D. and Griffin, S. (1996) Quality for the under threes, in G. Pugh (ed.) *Contemporary Issues in the Early Years*, 2nd edn. London: Paul Chapman/Sage.

Wachs, T. (2000) Nutritional deficits and behavioural development, *International Journal of Behavioural Development*, 24(4): 435–41.

Webster-Stratton, C. (1999) *How to Promote Children's Social and Emotional Competence*. London: Paul Chapman Publishing.

9 'Arty Farty Nonsense?': Working with Parents in the Art Gallery

Rachel Holmes

> through growing up in a particular culture, children acquire the
> social practices that have been attached to different emotions and
> refined through dominant social constructions ... practitioners need
> therefore to have parents relate to them well and to help them
> understand their child's and their family's particular patterns of
> behaviour and customs ...
> (Kamel and Dockrell 2000, cited in David *et al.* 2003: 53)

This chapter reflects upon Kamel and Dockrell's words and attempts to
highlight the complexities, dilemmas and challenges we encountered in relation to their claims when a group of professionals worked with parents and
their young children in an art gallery context. In this chapter I reflect upon
why we considered working with parents to be a valuable practice, but also
how we were led to conclude that established assumptions and misconcep-
tions made and held by professionals acted to inhibit fuller parental involvement. The chapter attempts to recognize our efforts as professionals in
this context and offers comments on observed practices that seemed to
constrain contributions made by parents. It also looks to identify possible
ways of addressing some of the challenging issues that were encountered in
this process.

The *Birth to Three Matters* framework (DfES 2002) is underpinned by ten
principles, seven of which manifest a direct relationship with our art gallery
project and the reflections upon that project throughout this chapter.

Parents and families are central to the well-being of the child

With the increasing recognition of parental expertise in relation to their
own children, there is a current move in out-of-home settings to work more
proactively with parents as partners (Whalley 2001: 12). This approach
tends to stress the complementary roles that different adults play in

children's lives. However, I would argue that this is not always an approach manifested within relationships between adults who live and work with children.

Researchers from the Early Years and Arts Education centres at Manchester Metropolitan University (MMU) developed a partnership project with Manchester Art Gallery (MAG) to include young children and their parents in creative experiences over a three-month period, based in the art gallery. A central theme became the tensions within emerging relationships between the children, their parents, early years practitioners, artists, art gallery educators and the research team. In this chapter, I will be focusing upon parental involvement as parents assumed different and changing roles, including those of observer, participator, 'expert', learner and facilitator. With reference to *Birth to Three Matters: A Review of the Literature* (David *et al.* 2003) and other recent theoretical perspectives collated by two research students working on the project (MacRae and Matsoukari-Stylianou 2004), I intend to reflect upon the ways in which as researchers we were able to attend to 'lost moments', notice the quiet comments and observe how the parents' shifting roles began to allow for them to become more active subjects within emerging multi-professional relationships.

Relationships with other people

Relationships became a central feature as our project progressed, manifesting themselves in a multiplicity of intricate and more overt ways. I use the term 'relationship' here to include the range of interactions that seemed to emerge between all those involved, for example children, parents/carers, setting practitioners, artists, art gallery educators and the research team. The notion of building and nurturing relationships also grew to infer connections that the children and parents were understood to make, both on conceptual and emotional levels, and ways in which the different spaces designated as learning contexts: the nursery, the gallery, and the education studio became inter-relational in their provision and stimulus for creative experiences with young children. In order to explore how the differing relationships found form and expression, we focused upon two generic areas:

- shifting and re-conceptualizing roles (expert, observer, participator, facilitator);
- expressions of emotionality and learning socially.

Parents' shifting and re-conceptualizing roles

Robinson suggests that 'Creativity is not a purely individual process; even working alone the individual draws from the ideas, achievements and influences of other people' (2001: 166–7), and throughout the project the nature of the different and changing relationships became a key factor in the way the children and parents engaged with the art gallery and studio materials. The parents voices emerged as 'experts', observers, participators, learners and facilitators and we observed the dynamics of these shifting roles as their levels of confidence, enthusiasm, motivation, interest and involvement changed.

The parents seemed to assume different and changing responsibilities, of which there were many examples. It was observed that at the outset of the sessions, some parents seemed to opt for what could be described as a 'back seat' role, choosing to stand back and remain a non-participant observer, their presence seeming non-active, yet crucially important. We did not consider this unusual given the unfamiliar context and range of 'professional' adults who seemed to dominate the art gallery experience. In an attempt to move parents into a more comfortable position, we encouraged them to take part in activities with their child.

In recognition of how the *Birth to Three Matters* framework makes suggestions for 'effective practice', we were mindful of how we might, 'use different voices to tell stories and get young children to join in wherever possible, sometimes using puppets, soft toys or real objects as "props" … ' (DfES 2002). We specifically used a range of storytelling moments, sitting in front of large paintings and with the use of 'props' engaged children and their parents. When the artist and educator guided the children through the gallery it was observed that they were supported in language and explanations by parents and practitioners, significant connections being made by parents, and children's own life experiences informing the storytelling. A very interesting flow of 'expertise' emerged within the storytelling moments that in its entirety became interactional in support of the totality of the experience. The following extract demonstrates how this fluidity and the intensity of the shared storytelling moments were observed in context by a practitioner and one of the research team:

> *Practitioner*: [child] connects bubbles to painting [14.6.64. by John Hoyland] … noticed and articulated by parent … artist used word 'background' … the children didn't understand, then used the children's own T-shirts to talk about colour which they seemed very engaged with, it seemed to connect them and the picture in a very concrete way …
> (Evaluation Report 2004)

This extract suggests the importance of parental knowledge of the child and the significance of their voice among professionals who may miss key opportunities that the children present. Another example is the way in which parents became linguistic mediators and advocates for their child's voice. A mother, herself a confident art gallery user and French speaker, conversed with her daughter throughout in French, exploring more complicated ideas in the child's first and more developed language and thus enabling her daughter's fuller engagement with the whole experience. Although art could be perceived to transcend language, the child's mother may have felt she wanted her daughter to more fully experience what was being said in relation to the works of art and perhaps she wanted to share her own experiences in her first language. There are many implications for practitioners here. It seems that increasingly multi-racial, multi-religious, multi-cultural and multi-linguistic early years contexts have much to learn about being proactive in promoting inclusive practices which celebrate and build on diversity as opposed to assimilation. Taking this observation into consideration, 'according to Siraj-Blatchford and Clarke's (2000: 30) review of research on bilingualism, there are many advantages to being exposed to more than one language from birth ... ' (David *et al.* 2003: 78), including self-esteem, positive identity and attitudes towards language learning. They add that even when the young child has gone to nursery, it is important they still have 'opportunities to carry on developing home language because it is the strength of this that provides the basis for the additional language ... ' (2003: 78).

It was noted that not only did parents offer bilingual support but they also mediated for their child when they felt the child's expressions were not being heard, alerting the group to their attempts to participate – evident in the following discussion: ' ... it's nice to have her [parent] there ... you know the girls aren't that vocal ... she's very supportive in that sense ... she made sure that they knew, that we knew, at least, that they were saying something ... you don't hear, and it gets drowned out ... ' (Evaluation Report 2004).

Another parent responded to a child herself, realizing the artist was busy talking with another child: ' "Look at this ... look at this!" [child trying to show artist his circle in Clore Interactive Gallery]. Parent responded and acknowledged his efforts' (transcribed extract from video footage).

Again, these examples foreground the importance of working more collaboratively with parents as 'experts' and 'facilitators' and the need for practitioners to encourage and support parents in their contributions, recognizing the principle that 'children learn most effectively when, with the support of a knowledgeable and trusted adult, they are enabled to be actively involved' (DfES 2002).

Throughout each of the sessions, parents, some of whom had seemed initially reserved, became more proactive as they positioned themselves as facilitators and enablers, and also seemed drawn into the creative process at their own level:

> I found making the spirals using the wax interesting.
> (Parental questionnaire)

> If we put paint on the paper then the spinning top will scrape the surface and make circle patterns.
> (Parent)

Here we observed a parent feeling confident enough to extend the activities on offer in the Education Studios. We regarded this as a very positive and enriching moment when the parent, knowing how her child responded to and enjoyed activities, was able to approach the gallery educator to build on the creative experience. On reflection, this led us to think about ways of extending parental involvement into the initial planning stages of the project, which is something we would endeavour to do in future sessions.

One question posed in the questionnaire was 'Have you any suggestions about how to improve the art gallery experience for you?' and one parent responded, 'Let the parents make something as well!' This suggests that despite some parents becoming absorbed in activities, others had either misread our signals, in that they were unsure as to whether they were invited to participate or not, or were embedded within an already established role in relation to home/nursery, parent/professional expectations and subsequently had positioned themselves outside the learning and creative processes. Although all parents were invited to partake, at a covert level, this is certainly an issue for the gallery educators/artists to consider, as it was noticeable how parents from each of the three settings involved in the study all responded differently to the entire experience. This might suggest something about the usual nursery/home interface and established relationships with and expectations of parents, as well as more generic political issues concerning 'partnerships' between parents and professionals. For some, home/nursery liaisons are purely pragmatic and functional, founded on a 'need to know' basis, whereas for others there is a sense of fuller participation within an evolving partnership that is more meaningful, interactive, fluid and collaborative. Importantly, the nature and manifestation of this crucial relationship between home and nursery helps to negotiate and mediate the often disparate worlds which the young child is asked to transcend. Barnett suggests, 'the children are often subjected to very different routines, ways of communicating and values at home and at nursery' (1995: 225). Similarly, when home/nursery come together and one community finds itself immersed and struggling to find a voice within another, Bhatti poses the question, 'How do they [children] make sense of their world and of different aspects of their daily lives: what do they make of … teachers' and parents' views?' (1999: 1). Edwards and Knight recognize that there is a clear demarcation in the balance of power that exists between home and institutional settings (1997: 65). This became a significant area of focus for us and one that led us to begin thinking about ways to recognize and work with different 'communities of practice' (Wenger 1998) and the power imbalances that seem to emerge when different communities and practices come together.

In relation to the significance of these issues for the gallery project, the idea of 'communities of practice' and ways in which these established 'practices' and associated identities transfer into different situations and contexts raise a host of issues, as the gallery may have to be much more explicit as to their own desires and aspirations for the parental experience. It could be argued that practices that are family-based are already nego- tiated, constrained and at best compromised within any institutional context, so it is all the more important to consider what might be the emotional and practical impact on the children, parents, practitioners and gallery staff when the inhabitants of these two worlds find themselves thrown together within a new space and are expected to work in a cohesive and cooperative way. Even though we recognized this as an issue em- bedded within an evolving, long-term commitment to working with par- ents, we did consider ways to nurture greater communication between parents and professionals within this project. We discussed how future sessions might:

- include parents at the initial planning stages;
- offer parent 'training days' to experience the gallery and pieces of art for themselves before working with the children;
- encourage parents to have greater input and participation in the gallery and studio sessions;
- offer weekend family workshops to nurture more frequent visits.

Expressions of emotionality and learning socially

The principles expressed in the *Birth to Three Matters* framework convey that babies and young children are social beings, that they are primed to learn and communicate and that learning is a shared process. David *et al.* (2003: 52) suggest that:

> Kamel and Dockrell (2000) found that mothers' interpretation of their babies' facial expressions as indicative of different emotional states varied according to the situational context, whereas the in- terpretations of observers who were not familiar with the babies did

not, indicating how emotional intimacy promotes shared understandings ...

This quotation, together with the principle noted above highlight the importance of professionals working alongside parents, as they clearly have a wealth of experience and understanding of their child that could be accessed within out-of-home contexts. The *Birth to Three Matters* framework suggests that effective practice involves adults responding to and building on babies' and young children's actions, expressions and gestures, which helps them become confident learners. By building upon the potential relationship between practitioners and parents, the breadth and sensitivity of responses to children's actions, expressions and gestures could be greatly enhanced.

Throughout our project we noted how the parents' confidence in their children, alongside the other adults, encouraged sustained interest in complex pieces of art. On reflection, it seemed unhelpful to second-guess the art pieces that children and their parents might have been interested in, to ghettoize their potential 'family' experiences, yet how we went about selecting pieces of art, by finding what it might be that appealed to young children and their parents, seemed significant in the education department's task of providing experiences that engage children and parents on many levels. Another issue we considered was whether it is the qualities or dynamics of particular art pieces that appeal to children, or the way in which the children are brought to the piece and taken through it by the parents, gallery educator and artist. The notion of who children take the journey with through the gallery, as well as the particulars of the route they take are areas that have also thrown up fascinating contemplations in the form of: the presence of parents; the previous experiences of the practitioners in relation to gallery visits; the familiarity of the children with the building and the intricacies of the social interactions as the children, parents, practitioners and artist travel through the spaces, making connections, feeling and touching the experiences as they do so.

Within the project, one observation raised our awareness of differing interpretations and expectations of the children and the role of their parents, since in their desire to provide emotional support, parents seemed comfortable expressing physical closeness with their children, and perhaps this was reciprocated as the children seemed similarly to reassure and reaffirm their parents' role in an unfamiliar environment:

I watched her a lot, and she was the only child that wasn't completely engaged ... then I noticed you [to practitioner] got her away from mum and she was becoming involved ... trying to step in ... and separate more ... mum wants them both to do the same thing ...

(Researcher, from transcript)

We incorporated parents as a positive thing ... but this is another side of it, the impact they can have on the children ...

(Researcher, from transcript)

However, observations noting this close physical contact, in addition to comments made in the post-session evaluation, yielded discussions for future consideration.

This issue raises further interesting dilemmas for 'professionals' in relation to Greenhalgh's suggestion that 'Children's self-confidence is affected and influenced by the way adults respond to them ... ' (1994: 12). Given that there were a number of 'adults' who responded in very different ways to the children – parents, practitioners, artists, gallery educator – it is assumed that they all responded according to their differentiated, yet interrelated roles, with different sets of understandings, value systems, specific agendas and intentions. These were difficult and sensitive observations and our interpretations of the term 'clingy' left us rethinking why we felt this was deficit behaviour. Why had we described it as 'clingy' and why, within this context, did we feel it was inappropriate? Having to reconsider our assumptions and expectations of children and their parents was a useful practice in preparation for reconfiguring how we might approach similar behaviours in the future. We recognized that professional discourses construct parents and their designated roles in particular ways within the gallery. Some parents were 'being' with their children in a way that seems to have been perceived as 'stifling' or as exhibiting 'domineering and restrictive' behaviours (as the extracts from the transcripts suggest). Professional ideologies espousing child-centred, autonomous, self-directed and active learning might empathize with the tension clearly communicated within these observations. I ponder for a moment how we might begin to resolve what seems to be a conflict of interests. As professionals, do we make judgements about what is in the best 'educational' interests of the child, even if that silences the parents' voice? How do we interpret the parents' agenda, do we stand in judgement of cultural and familial practices that seem to raise questions about the emotional relationships within which we operate, particularly when faced with the home/out-of-home interface? To position this dilemma within a framework offered by Greenhalgh (1994) the genesis is the point at which all these internal and external influences, such as past and present experiences, experience of family, culture and friends and inter- and intra-personal experience come together – the child.

It was important to experience the children in relation to the past and present influences that surround them and the parents were considered a significant link within this endeavour. The *Birth to Three Matters* principles suggest that young children's lives are not split up into sections and argue that neither should their adult carers divide their lives up into segments, so although any kind of pseudo-divisions within a child's life could be interpreted as being simplistic in relation to the holistic and shifting experiences of the child, Greenhalgh's ideas are useful here in that they suggest that there is a web of intricate intra-personal and inter-relational processes that embed each individual child within any particular context. It is through the nature of these inter-relational processes that a child could be perceived as growing to understand who they are and developing a sense of belonging. We recognize that a child's predominant sense of identity and belonging will usually be embedded within their immediate family, rooted within complex cultural and familial messages. The project acknowledged that within this are a diversity of dominant voices, some of which emerge from, and are communicated through academia, filtering into policy and practice. Academia, theoretical ideologies and practitioners assert a particular view of what is regarded as appropriate 'independent learning' behaviours for the developing Strong Child, while also positioning 'others' (here any non-compliant parents) as 'outsiders', as 'overprotective' or 'interfering'. Yet when home meets setting, the established boundaries become messily transcended. This interface creates a tension, where children may manifest home-like behaviours, responded to by parents, which could be perceived by professionals as signs of insecurity or dependency and the parents as controlling or alternatively not firm enough:

> And it's also, you feel a bit ... embarrassed disciplining the child when the mother's there. I know there was one little girl, in particular, who was quite vociferous ... a little bit overpowering, I thought ...
> (Practitioner, post-session evaluation)

> I didn't think those children that I brought would be 'clingy'. That was an experience for me cos they're quite confident, we chose quite confident children in the nursery, so for them to be 'clingy' like that ... I didn't expect that ...
> (Practitioner, post-session evaluation)

The project team were aware of the range of interpretations placed on varying parental attitudes and behaviours towards their children. It is at the centre of these complex dilemmas that this project positions the negotiation of the role and expectations of the different adults. Whose definition of a Strong Child do we mean? Whose do we use? Whose do we perceive as the absolute in educational terms? As gallery staff and as trainers, we need to be aware of how we construct parents, what we assume of them and of their relationships with professionals in their child's setting. We need to consider, negotiate and certainly be explicit in stating how much we would like them to contribute and participate in sessions such as the gallery session, but we need also to be mindful of the ways in which they feel they are able to access and engage (with our encouragement), being sensitive to the different ways in which they take part and build on the strengths they bring to the experience.

Out of this project has emerged the sustained interest of a number of parents in developing their own confidence and understanding of an art gallery as a context for learning, and this has become the basis for MMU's ongoing collaboration with MAG, as we develop the second phase of the project. This phase focuses on gaining professional insights into ways in which parents' confidence, self-esteem and knowledge can be nurtured, built upon and supported through the provision of creative experiences. We are making a concerted effort to include both mothers and fathers, culturally, racially and religiously diverse families, and different and same-sex parents. We will also examine the relationship between building parents' confidence to partake in creative activities and the positive influence this could have on their abilities to support their children's creative development and find ways to build relationships between culturally diverse local communities and public galleries in the pursuit of this learning. The project has also given rise to the development of continued professional development opportunities for professionals and a particular focus concerns negotiating different ways of working with parents.

On a final note, the contributions parents made to the experience was substantial. The team's differing interpretations of their role and how parents themselves had understood their participation necessitated some difficult decisions. We have had to rethink how we invite parents to partake and how we might encourage them to do this. It is clear that the gallery will be providing early years sessions to many different settings, all of whom will have very diverse relationships with parents, and on this basis we intend to be directive in terms of the role we would want them to take. Parents will be invited to participate in the capacity of facilitator and supporter of the children's explorations in the gallery and studio. The potential of training for parents/carers who might want to know more about how they can use the gallery in their child's creative development might support their understanding of this role, but for those who do not want to, or cannot take up the training, the preparation pack sent to settings will clarify the nature of parental involvement. This decision in itself seems prescriptive and makes me consider how, when one person is competent, their abilities may often inhibit others. It has become increasingly clear that these early years sessions are primarily for the *children*, with parents in a supportive and contributory role. By directing parents towards the role we wanted them to adopt, we were not intending to negate their competencies, but to provide a multi-professional pedagogical approach which they felt they could confidently and actively contribute to. However, we also recognize that the journey to transcend expectations and proactively bridge the gap between the parents', practitioners' and artists' 'knowledge' of the child may be the genesis for a revitalized sense of partnership. Both parents and practitioners seem to have been able to see the children in different ways and what we take from this experience is important in the preparation for, and implementation of, future art gallery sessions.

References

Barnett, L. (1995) What is good day care? in J. Trowell and M. Bower (eds) *The Emotional Needs of Children and their Families*. London: Routledge.

Bhatti, G. (1999) Asian Children at Home and at School. London: Routledge.

David, T., Goouch, K., Powell, S. and Abbott, L. (2003) *Birth to Three Matters: A Review of the Literature*. London: DfES Publications.

DfES (2002) *Birth to Three Matters*. London: DfES Publications.

Edwards, A. and Knight, P. (1997) Parents and professionals, in B. Costin and M. Hales (eds) *Families, Education and Social Differences*. London: Routledge.

Greenhalgh, P. (1994) *Emotional Growth and Learning*. London: Routledge.

Holmes, R. and Sohel, J. (2004) *Young Children in the Art Gallery*. Unpublished evaluation report.

Kamel, H. and Dockrell, J.E. (2000) Divergent perspectives, multiple meanings: a comparison of care-givers' and observers' interpretations of infant behaviour, *Journal of Reproductive and Infant Psychology*, 18(1): 41–60.

MacRae, C. and Matsoukari-Stylianou, C. (2004) Review of literature, in R. Holmes and J. Sohel (eds) *Young Children in the Art Gallery*. Unpublished evaluation report.

Robinson, K. (2001) *Out of Our Minds: Learning to be Creative*. London: Copstone Press.

Siraj-Blatchford, I. and Clarke, P. (2000) *Supporting Identity, Diversity and Language in the Early Years*. Buckingham: Open University Press.

Wenger, E. (1998) *Communities of Practice: Learning, Meaning and Identity*. London: Cambridge University Press.

Whalley, M. (2001) *Involving Parents in their Children's Learning*. London: Paul Chapman.

10 Special Lives: Working with Parents of Children with Special Educational Needs and Disabilities

Julie Jennings

It is widely accepted that parents are children's first and most enduring educators, playing a crucial role in the education of their children. There is a wealth of research evidence to suggest that children do better when

- There is a close working relationship between home and setting
- Information about children's learning is shared between everyone involved in the child's learning and development
- Parents show a keen interest in their children's education and make learning part of everyday life.

(DfES 2005)

The above quotation is taken from the introduction to *Foundation Stage Parents: Partners in Learning* (DfES 2005), which has been developed to identify and disseminate effective practice in parental partnership. The philosophy it embraces permeates *Birth to Three Matters* (DfES 2002) and this approach to working with parents should apply equally to parents who have a child with special educational needs (SEN) or a disability. The reasons for working with parents are the same:

> the power of parents to participate as equal partners in the cyclical process of assessment, provision and review stems from the relationship they share with the child. It is a relationship at the heart of early development which crosses artificial divides between care and education.

(Jones 2004: 99)

The principle that 'parents and families are central to the well being of the child' is the filter for *Birth to Three Matters* which offers the opportunity to include parents in a framework of effective practice that can support them and their child. This framework includes all children: *Birth to Three Matters* provides the context for sharing thoughts and ideas about young children's development and learning, including children with SEN or a disability.

Historically, the family-focused approach has been slower to develop in the field of early childhood special education because the focus has been primarily on the child and their needs, rather than services for the whole family (Wilson 1998: 142). Parents should be viewed as experts on their child, equivalent and complementary to those who have other expertise to offer. *The Code of Practice on the Identification and Assessment of Special Educational Needs* (DfES 2001) contains a whole chapter dedicated to working in partnership with parents. This includes a requirement to establish Parent Partnership Schemes which may be linked to the work of area special educational needs coordinators (SENCOs). It states that 'parents hold key information and have a critical role to play in their children's education. They have unique strengths, knowledge and experience to contribute to the shared view of a child's needs and the best ways of supporting them' (DfES 2001: 16).

However, the population of children with SEN and disability is diverse and includes a growing number of children with significant continuing additional needs: these children and their families often require a high level of long-term support. For instance, the report of the British Childhood Visual Impairment Study Group (Rahi and Cable 2003) found that visually impaired children are now more likely to:

- have been premature;
- be of South Asian origin;
- have associated neurological problems;
- have a condition which is not treatable;
- have had their condition from very early life;
- have similarly affected siblings;
- be from areas of disadvantage.

Other factors such as unemployment and poverty are more prevalent in families with a disabled child and there is evidence of difficulties for these families in accessing services (Daycare Trust 2001). Other research has shown that the combination of disadvantaged circumstances and difficulties in securing access to appropriate services, which are found for the majority of families with a disabled child, are particularly acute for families from minority ethnic groups (Fazil *et al.* 2002).

For parents who have a child with SEN or a disability, this may initiate a process which leads from involving parents to supporting parenting, to creating parents as professionals. Parents may become therapist, nurse, teacher, manager, advocate – all of which may alter their daily relationship with their child:

> For most families, looking after their children at home meant that they had to organize family life around the children's care. The special requirements for this often left little room for 'ordinary' family life. Parts of the home might have had to be turned into extensions of the hospital, even containing professional carers, and the parents themselves became the providers and managers of a wide range of technical procedures. They sometimes even felt that professionals taught them these as if they were clinic staff, to the extent that the professionals concentrated on teaching the technical aspects of care and neglected the emotional impact of the tasks on the parents.
>
> (Quinton 2004: 109)

This professionalization of parenting can be damaging for some parents. Parents are the natural environment for their child, a resource for their child. They have what has been called '24-hour knowledge' of their child; but what may this mean for them?

Including families

The focus on very young children enabled by *Birth to Three Matters* means that any support for the child must be mediated through the family. David Quinton's research shows that, for families with a child with SEN or disability, access to informal support is limited: 'it was clear that the special skills and knowledge needed to care for the children limited the practical support that family and friends could give. They were often not able to babysit, take the children out or pick them up from school' (2004: 111). For some parents this can lead to a feeling that there is 'no time for us' (Contact a Family 2004). Limitations on informal support may throw parents back on professional resources for early education and care. This is often, and particularly for children from birth to 3 years, described as 'early intervention'.

The 'articles of faith' regarding early intervention were questioned more than 20 years ago by Michael Davis when he remarked that we need to be sure 'that we are not simply taking action for the sake of doing something which looks purposeful, that we are not conveying a message to parents that only by special techniques can their children develop adequately' (Davis 1984: 8). Much has evolved in this field over this period, and for many parents early intervention is important, but we should not assume that it is essential for all.

However, Philippa Russell gives two broad-based definitions of early intervention which show that an inclusive approach for a range of family needs is possible:

> Early intervention can be defined as all forms of child orientated training activities and parent orientated guidance activities which are implemented in direct and immediate consequence of the identification of the developmental condition. Early intervention pertains to the child as well as to the parents, the family and the broader social network. Early intervention can include play, family support, early education, and appropriate health care, anything which supports the child's development. Early intervention is best conceptualized as a system designed to support family patterns of interaction that best promote children's development and optimize their access to, and use of, educational and other services which are usually provided for children in their community.
>
> (Russell 2004: 4)

The aim of early intervention is to support families to support their children's development, to promote children's coping confidence (Wolfendale 2000: 14).

Barnett *et al.* (1998) describe how interventions may be viewed on a continuum of intrusiveness, from radical changes to interventions that fit, or may be adapted to, existing styles of parenting. They advocate a form of environmental intervention: naturalistic interventions which are based on the actual roles, routines, skills and interests of children and caregivers. This mirrors the principles of *Birth to Three Matters* where learning builds on planned and incidental experiences within the context of a caring relationship, following the child's lead.

Success depends on both valuing and supporting parents in their parenting role as part of any intervention programme, since 'if parents do not feel respected, they are unlikely to engage well with a programme' (DfES 2004: 119). This view is confirmed by Dale, who argues that early intervention will, in the longer term, be unlikely to succeed without active partnership with families, and advocates a negotiating model of partnership: 'a working relationship where the partners use negotiation and joint decision-making and resolve differences of opinion and disagreement in order to reach some kind of shared perspective or jointly agreed decision on issues of mutual concern' (1996: 14).

Wilson supports this view, outlining some of the critical features which define effective early intervention programmes. This includes the view that professionals work with parents as full partners in educational planning and decision-making and, in the process, recognize and support a variety of family structures and priorities (Wilson 1998: 6).

Effective early intervention also depends on the availability of relevant and accessible information on which parents are enabled to make decisions about their own, and their children's, lives. Research found that:

> information about parenting reaches parents in many different ways, and there is no single channel which reaches them all ... All parents turn to and feel happiest obtaining information from sources they trust ... this usually means local contacts with the universal services
>
> (Eborall and Garmeson 2001: 11)

However, for parents with disabled children, this is more likely to be targeted services: professionals are the most common source of information and this comes mainly through personal contact.

As practitioners, we need to ensure that both universal and targeted services are readily available to families as needed. Cowen suggests that 'as families caring for disabled children we need support services geared to our individual family's needs right from the very early days after diagnosis. Most families prefer services integrated with those for other children and families' (2002: 11). This active role of the parents of disabled children is paramount to give them back a sense of control:

> their service needs may be very specialized and specific but, as far as the parents are concerned, one purpose of these inputs should be to allow them to care for their children themselves. They want to stay in control of their lives and solve problems in their own way.
>
> (Quinton 2004: 108)

Information is acknowledged as a vital component for parents in understanding the practical implications of their child's disability. It is needed 'on an ongoing basis to furnish parents with sufficient knowledge of the child's condition so they could plan meaningfully and hence feel in control of their families' life' (Pain 1999: 310). But access to timely and appropriate information is one of the three specific problems in terms of formal support which David Quinton (2004: 111–12) highlights:

- information;
- equipment and medication;
- short-term care and home support.

These problems can be reduced by effective organization of formal support – through inter-agency working and key working systems – which maintain parents' own sense of control and build upon their strengths.

What works?

Effective inter-agency working is a significant factor for families, as these comments by parents illustrate: 'so many people wanted to know our business'; 'that's what makes it so difficult – we're having to fit in with everyone else's professional boundaries'. The role of a key worker across agencies is pivotal in making sure that interventions work for parents. One parent described a key worker 'like having a big cushion to buffer you from all the inconsequential things that go on in your life . . . a cushion is a buffer but also a comfort'.

Research has shown (Greco *et al.* 2005: viii) that the best outcomes for families are achieved when the role of key worker includes:

- providing information to families about services and support available, both locally and nationally, and how to access these;
- providing information about the child's condition where needed;
- identifying and addressing the needs of all family members;
- coordinating care and supporting families with care planning and review;
- improving access to services;
- providing emotional support;
- providing help and support in a crisis.

These are the principles that underpin the Care Coordination Network UK Key Worker Standards which are endorsed in the *National Service Framework for Children, Young People and Maternity Services* (DoH 2004).

Parental satisfaction with services is strongly influenced by the perception that services are more family-centred (Law *et al.* 2003), where families feel an ownership of those services. Services should be:

- responsive to needs;
- culturally sensitive;
- respect[ful of] the parents' expertise on their own problems (Quinton 2004: 132).

These factors should be set in the context of professionals' acknowledging their own expertise and using it positively in providing services to families: 'in the broadest sense, family-centredness means having cultural sensitivity to families. Professionals can be culturally sensitive to families without having to relinquish their expertise' (Brorson 2005: 72). These factors are embedded in the *Early Support Programme* (DfES 2003).

Early support

In an editorial discussing how health professionals might best disclose a child's disability to the parents, Bax (2002: 579) suggests that it is a lifetime task:

> Disability is not a tidy subject, and untidiness and muddle is not just something that parents suffer, but it's something that professionals suffer too as they struggle to try and form a satisfactory information network throughout the child's early life and into adolescence and adult life. Disclosure is not a task over and done with. It continues.

Difficulties may have been recognized at birth, or there may be a growing awareness of differences or delays in development, either by parents or others who know the child. How the news of a disability is shared with parents has been shown to subsequently affect their views of relations with professionals. In the words of one parent: 'it stays with you for the rest of your life'. Addressing this critical issue researchers stress that it is important to understand that 'the experience of this group of parents, and the context in which they are parenting, may be different from that of a family with a non-disabled child' (Dickins and Denziloe 2003: 95). Parents may feel alienated by their experiences, particularly if they receive or express negative feelings about the disability itself. The parent of a young child with Down's syndrome, Claire Edwards says 'that parents generally enter the world of special needs unwillingly and with some trepidation' (2002: 5).

Every family is different, and so it is important that practitioners are able to work in diverse ways. Wilson describes the 'unique demands and stressors' that having a disabled child can place on a family: 'the presence of such demands and stressors, however, does not make the family dysfunctional, heroic, or incompetent; nor does it make all families with children with disabilities alike' (Wilson 1998: 143–4). She concludes that parents should be given options for when, how and to what extent they wish to be involved. This may include the option of not being involved, which should be allowed and respected. However, she confirms that 'an important concept to keep in mind is that not being involved with their child's program does not mean that parents are not involved with their child' (Wilson 1998: 146).

There is also diversity in parental responses to disability. Parents for Inclusion (2002: 6), in *Welcoming All Children Into The World*, set out their vision for an ideal world where there is no:

- antenatal testing;
- prejudice;

- targets of 'normality';
- developmental checklists;
- brain grading;
- medical model of disability.

Anyone working with very young disabled children and their families should not make assumptions about how parents may respond to the birth of their child or view the services offered. Wall suggests also that 'parental involvement and participation are susceptible to change as children progress through the educational phases' (2003: 44). She highlights that, in the early days, the transfer to an early years setting may require sensitive handling as the 'parent/carer may feel even more protective and find it much harder to transfer their child's care over to others' (2003: 45).

In an attempt to introduce more effective practice in the area of sharing the news and in subsequent support, the DoH and DfES jointly issued practical guidance for professionals working with disabled children from birth to third birthday. This publication, *Together from the Start* (DfES and DoH 2003) gives key messages about:

- effective multi-agency family support;
- involvement of families in planning and delivery of services;
- better information to parents so that they are aware of the support services that are available and what statutory services should be delivered;
- developing the role of key workers;
- better training to improve professional knowledge and skills;
- agreed joint family support plans;
- better networking between agencies and knowledge of what works well and where.

To help promote these messages, the DfES established the *Early Support Programme* (DfES 2003). *Early Support* and *Birth to Three Matters* are the twin support mechanisms for children from birth to 3 years with SEN or a disability: *Early Support* provides the pathway and *Birth to Three Matters* the vehicle.

The outcomes of the *Early Support Programme* are materials to:

- support professionals in service delivery;
- support and inform families;
- audit how services work with parents and other agencies;
- track progress in deaf and other children.

But, as proponents of the *Early Support Programme* state, the materials are *not* the intervention. In the end, 'how parenting support is delivered may matter more than what is delivered' (DfES 2004: 120) because 'relationships lie at the heart of support' (Quinton 2004: 130). As explained by one parent:

When you are looking after a child with a disability, this can be a very lonely journey because nobody else is in that situation with you. So it helps to have someone to listen to your frustrations and concerns and help you understand that you are doing your best as a person.

This has been described as 'becoming an ally' (Dickins and Denziloe 2003: 98). Relationships between parents and professionals are central to successful partnership working, but this may be challenged if the *parent* has a disability.

Discussing parenting with a disability, Olsen and Tyers (2004: 31) warn:

It is inappropriate to talk about disabled parents having a special set of needs for support; rather, that disabled parents need what all parents need in order to parent successfully ... What is different is that many of these sources of support are less easily accessed by disabled parents: the focus, therefore, should be on breaking down barriers to disabled parents accessing these mainstream supports.

Disabled parents do report difficulties in many practical aspects of parenting: making up bottles, changing nappies, administering medicine, recognizing when the child is ill – or has nits. But they also report difficulties with the attitudes of some professionals: one prospective father commented that 'having to effectively train a couple of dozen people in visual impairment awareness at this stressful time isn't much fun; even simple things like asking midwives and doctors to make clear who they were and what they were doing during the birth was a losing battle'. Another mother stated: 'I was not treated as an adult [professionals] talked through relatives who were perceived as my carers'.

In addition, disabled parents have noted that:

- services often concentrated on the parents' disability and ignored their needs as parents;
- parenting was sometimes not seen as a legitimate support need;
- services made assumptions or demands about the partners' ability to care (Quinton 2004: 129). Quinton concludes that 'for disabled parents as well as parents of disabled children, relationships with family and friends were complicated by problems of balance of help and its availability, as well as understanding and tolerance of the impairment' (p. 130).

Some of the key issues for disabled parents are reported as:

- access to information;
- one size does not fit all;
- support which fits in with family life;
- staying in control;
- the personal qualities of key professionals;
- someone fighting your corner;
- support that is flexible;
- support that is culturally appropriate;
- support that is timely and responsive;
- support that is imaginative (Olsen and Tyers 2004: 38–46).

Being imaginative and creative is important. For instance, one setting developed a 'walking bus' – a safe organized walk to the setting by children supervised by parents – which overcame one father's difficulties, as a wheel-chair user, in accompanying his child to school. The 'walking bus' was also beneficial for other children and parents.

Including parents in *Birth to Three Matters*

Successive legislation has given the parents of children with SEN or a dis-ability increased rights to participation. However, these very rights can bring increased bureaucracy which parents can find more distressing than their child's disability. These rights are often set in the context of 'overcoming' impairment, 'improving' the child rather than enabling the parent to feel good about themselves and their child, and their role as parent. *Birth to Three Matters* offers a positive alternative. It is not a formal curriculum; there is no pass or fail. It embraces an approach which does not prescribe activities or targets, but supports practitioners in creating responsive environments for young children and emphasizes the importance of experiences for active learning. It can also support the early identification of a child whose devel-opment does not occur quite so readily or may be less predictable. This ap-proach is key for young children with SEN and disabilities so that the ethos of early years development, learning and teaching permeates the practice that surrounds them. Practitioners working with children with complex needs have found the *Birth to Three Matters* framework useful as a guide to areas where the children have skills and differing abilities. It has helped them to focus their observations on detailed aspects of learning which they can share with parents. This has in turn helped them to plan for the children as they progress through to the next stage of learning, building on information and advice from specialist support services.

Birth to Three Matters is helpful to parents and practitioners because it reaffirms the view that all children are competent and capable from birth, and – most importantly – it does *not* reinforce an absolute 'milestones' approach to development. It describes broad areas – from Heads Up, Lookers and Communicators to Walkers, Talkers and Pretenders – along which children can take their individual journey.

Birth to Three Matters encourages an individualized approach and provides a framework for practitioners to offer effective practice with a range of parents and children. Consider the case study for the component card A Healthy Child – Healthy Choices which offers a practical example of a parent and practitioner working together:

> Laura, a two and a half year old with severe learning difficulties, explores a length of chain during heuristic play. She repeatedly pulls it back and forwards across her mouth, constantly watching the adult and checking her response. When viewing this sequence on video, Laura's mum explained 'I know why she keeps on looking at you, she's waiting to see if you will react like I do, and say stop putting things in your mouth!'
>
> (DfES 2002)

This could now be used to develop ways of working with Laura's mum to make sure that experiences are shared on a regular basis in the future to support Laura's learning in home and setting.

Birth to Three Matters is there to support parents and practitioners for, as Taly-Ongan (2001) stresses, early childhood educators already possess essential characteristics for working with young disabled children. These include:

- a sound knowledge of child development which enables them to plan for all children in an age-appropriate framework;
- knowledge of developmental differences and the use of individual approaches;
- awareness of family values and cultural diversity, and regular effective contact with parents;
- creating naturalistic environments in settings that are child- and family-centred;
- flexibility in approach and ability to use lateral thinking in problem solving (Talay-Ongan 2001: 228).

And to conclude . . .

The fact that there has been such a substantial change in attitudes and practices in delivery of services to children with disabilities and their families deserves recognition, but not complacency. Early childhood service providers can unpack their unique preparation and skills in becoming critically important members of multidisciplinary early intervention teams.

Early childhood education has a long history of being committed to parent involvement and family support. Indeed, Chris Lloyd goes so far as to say that 'the principles which inform early education can be seen to provide for the whole of education a model of genuine inclusion' (1997: 172). *Birth to Three Matters* offers such a model and can help address some of the gaps in knowledge about what works. *What Works in Parenting Support?* (Moran *et al.* 2004) outlines some of these gaps.

Children's perspectives

There is very little research on the views of children 'as the ultimate recipients of enhanced parenting support' (DfES 2004: 115). What makes a difference to their experiences? We need to encourage practitioners to have confidence in seeking the views of disabled children from birth to 3 years as this is still seen as a challenge.

Siblings

There is also a particular issue relating to the brothers and sisters of children with SEN or a disability. How that special need is managed, such as unequal treatment or the hostile attitudes of others, will have a significant impact on the brother or sister, both in the long and short term. Although their specific needs have been recognized for a long while, support programmes have been limited.

Fathers

Most interventions predominantly serve women so 'we still cannot say we know about "parenting support" – rather, we mainly know about "supporting mothers"' (DfES 2004: 116). Fathers may be reluctant to ask for information, especially from professionals, and feel excluded by information which is perceived to be focused on mothers. The way that information is presented needs to take this into account.

Grandparents

In addition, we know very little about what it means for grandparents to have a grandchild with a disability (Hastings 2000). Grandparents report similar initial reactions to the birth of a disabled child, but there is little support available and many grandparents consider that professionals do not take into account the needs of the extended family; nor is there always full recognition of the positive relationships that grandparents can develop with the disabled child, and the natural support resource they can provide: 'it is important that professionals and families are sensitive to grandparents' roles within the family, but also that they recognize that grandparents too need support' (Hastings 2000: 13).

Diversity

Most research on interventions is concerned with white families: more information is still needed on issues of attracting and retaining ethnically diverse groups of parents and issues connected with how best to develop and adapt programmes to accommodate differing perspectives on what constitutes appropriate parenting (DfES 2004: 116).

Birth to Three Matters represents an agreed framework which provides the opportunity to address some of these issues. It gives a shared language in which to open a dialogue with parents and reach a mutual understanding of their child. It offers parents of disabled and non-disabled children, and the practitioners working with them, a context for belonging – not to compare their children's relative progress, but to follow an evidence-based approach to successfully supporting and extending children's development and learning.

When this approach incorporates the practice embedded in *Early Support* there is the potential to '"normalise" access to support as a universal right ... The message that it is not unusual to need support from time to time needs to be conveyed in policy rhetoric, to help increase rates of access, especially at critical points for early intervention' (DfES 2004: 10).

We need to review and reflect on our current practice and move towards improved practice that approaches this universal right – and is appropriately resourced as such – because:

> What makes it so hard to evaluate is that the real cost can only be assessed through establishing the cost of its absence: of families who are frustrated and dissatisfied and fail to be helped by the services on offer and therefore perceive themselves as unsupported. Partnership practice has a price – but can we as a society afford or justify the alternative?
>
> (Dale 1996: 307)

References

Barnett, D.W., Bell, S.H. and Carey, K.T. (1998) *Designing PreSchool Interventions.* New York: The Guilford Press.

Bax, M.C.O (2002) Editorial, *Developmental Medicine and Child Neurology*, 44(9): 579.

Brorson, K. (2005) The culture of a home visit in early intervention, *Journal of Early Childhood Research*, 3(1): 51–76.

Contact a Family (2004) *Relationships – No Time for Us*. Research report. London: CAF.

Cowen, A. (2002) *Taking Care*, 2nd edn. York: The Family Fund Trust.

Dale, N. (1996) *Working with Families of Children with Special Needs: Partnership and Practice*. London: Routledge.

Davis, M. (1984) Too special, too soon? *Special Education: Forward Trends*, 11(3): 6–8.

Daycare Trust (2001) *Ambitious for All: Rising to the Childcare Challenge for Children with Disabilities and Special Needs. Childcare for All Thinking Big 5*. London: Daycare Trust.

DfES (2001) *The Code of Practice on the Identification and Assessment of Special Educational Needs*. London: DfES Publications.

DfES (2002) *Birth to Three Matters*. London: DfES Publications.

DfES (2003) *Early Support Programme*. London: DfES Publications.

DfES (2004) *What Works in Parental Support? Research Report*. London: DfES Publications.

DfES (2005) *Foundation Stage Parents: Partners in Learning*. London: DfES Publications.

DfES and DoH (2003) *Together from the Start – Practical Guidance for Professionals Working with Disabled Children (Birth to Third Birthday) and their Families*. London: DfES/DOH.

Dickins, M. and Denziloe, J. (2003) *All Together: How to Create Inclusive Services for Disabled Children and their Families*, 2nd edn. London: National Children's Bureau.

DoH (2004) *National Service Framework for Children, Young People and Maternity Services*. London: DoH.

Eborall, C. and Garmeson, K. (2001) *Desk Research on Communicating to Parents*. London: Home Office Family Policy Unit.

Edwards, C. (2002) Meeting the information needs of parents of children with special needs, *Early Education*, 37: 5.

Fazil, Q., Bywaters, P., Ali, Z., Wallace, L. and Singh, G. (2002) Disadvantage and discrimination compounded: the experience of Pakistani and Bangladeshi parents of disabled children in the UK, *Disability and Society*, 17(3): 237–53.

Greco, V., Sloper, P., Webb, R. and Beecham, J. (2005) *An Exploration of Different*

Models of Multiagency Partnerships in Keyworker Services for Disabled Children: Effectiveness and Costs. Research Report. London: DfES Publications.

Hastings, R. (2000) The role of grandparents, *Eye Contact,* 27: 12–13.

Jones, C. A. (2004) *Supporting Inclusion in the Early Years.* Maidenhead: Open University Press.

Law, M., Hanna, S., King, G., Hurley, P., King, S., Kertoy, M. and Rosenbaum, P. (2003) Factors affecting family-centred service delivery for children with disabilities, *Child: Care, Health and Development,* 29(5): 357–66.

Lloyd, C. (1997) Inclusive education for children with special educational needs in the early years, in S. Wolfendale (ed.) *Meeting Special Needs in the Early Years.* London: David Fulton.

Moran, P., Ghate, D. and van der Merwe, A. (2004) *What Works in Parenting Support?* London: DfES Publications.

Olsen, R. and Tyers, H. (2004) *Think Parent: Supporting Disabled Adults as Parents.* London: National Family and Parenting Institute.

Pain, H. (1999) Coping with a child with disabilities from the parents' perspective: the function of information, *Child: Care, Health and Development,* 25(4): 299–312.

Parents for Inclusion (2002) *Welcoming All Children Into The World.* Unpublished consultation response.

Quinton, D. (2004) *Supporting Parents: Messages from Research.* London: Jessica Kingsley.

Rahi, J.S. and Cable, N. (2003) on behalf of the British Childhood Visual Impairment Study Group (BCVISG) Severe Visual Impairment and Blindness in Children in the UK, *Lancet,* 362 (October): 1359–65.

Russell, P. (2004) *Early Intervention in the UK: Current Policy and Practice and Implications for Future Research and Development Work,* in progress as part of the DfES/Mencap feasibility study, March.

Talay-Ongan, A. (2001) Early intervention: critical roles of early childhood service providers, *International Journal of Early Years Education,* 9(3): 220–8.

Wall, K. (2003) *Special Needs and Early Years: a Practitioner's Guide.* London: Paul Chapman.

Wilson, R.A. (1998) *Special Educational Needs in the Early Years.* London: Routledge.

Wolfendale, S. (ed.) (2000) *Special Needs in the Early Years: Snapshots of Practice.* London: Routledge-Falmer/OMEP.

11 'Observe More … Do Less': The Approaches of Magda Gerber to Parent Education

Sue Owen and Stephanie Petrie

It can be argued that, despite the rhetoric, 'parenting' is conceptualized in current socioeconomic policies primarily from the perspective of adults and the state rather than that of children. Many professionals suggest that 'poor parenting' produces children and young people who are antisocial, ineducable, violent and promiscuous (Bell *et al* 2004; BBC News 2005a, 2005b). This current emphasis on the social costs of 'poor parenting' leads to a focus, in policies and practices, on parental tasks amenable to measurement by government performance indicators rather than on the parent-child relationship which we will be discussing in greater detail later. While a relationship might be harder to measure in such positivist ways it is possible to judge its quality by close observation of the child. In this chapter we will outline the emphasis placed by the educationist Magda Gerber on relationship-based parent education that is founded on close observation of the child. First, however, we will consider the current emphasis on 'poor parenting', the measures being taken by the state to change parental behaviours and the impact of these on children. We will subsequently examine the approaches of Magda Gerber, child development theorist and practitioner, who worked in the USA from the early 1950s. These were based on the work of her friend and colleague, the Hungarian paediatrician and scientist, Emmi Pikler (Petrie and Owen 2005) and were developed initially by Pikler for children in residential care and later by Gerber for parent-infant education and daycare settings. The developing and unique relationship between a very young child and their parent or carer is supported and enhanced by attuning the adult to the non-verbal cues of the child through observation and assisted reflection. There is substantial evidence to suggest that parent/carer and child are able to establish a mutually satisfying relationship because the child is better understood (Petrie and Owen 2005). A child that is better understood is easier to care for as their needs are recognized and met efficiently and appropriately. The chapter will conclude by showing how the 'Gerber approach' is congruent with the philosophy underpinning *Birth to Three Matters* (DfES 2002) and its potential usefulness in the UK context. We will argue that two services in particular, daycare and family support services in the community including parent education, which are central to current strategies to support parents and their children, could benefit from the 'Gerber approach'.

Parents and the labour market

The increasing emphasis on 'parenting' in economic policies can be seen in the strategies encouraging poor parents into the workforce as the most effective way out of 'social exclusion' for them and their children (Social Exclusion Unit 2005). The employed parent appears to be conceptualized, therefore, as a better parent than the parent without paid 'work'. Indeed, gauging parental attitudes to employment forms part of the Common Assessment Framework (CAF) (DfES 2005b) for assessing parental capacity as discussed further below. This suggests that 'parenting' itself is not considered 'work' worthy of adequate state support despite the emphasis in current policies on the importance of parenting: 'Parents, carers and families are the most important influence on children and young people's outcomes' (DfES 2005a). Parents entering the labour market, especially lone parents and usually mothers, are heavily reliant on daycare yet there is substantial evidence to show that the supply of daycare is insufficient to meet demand and often unavailable at the times and in the places needed:

> I could not get childcare for those funny hours. I just couldn't get it. You can get nine to five and that's it, but because it was residential care, you go out in the morning and you go out in the evening ... And then I couldn't find a child carer, could not ... There isn't any, do you know what I mean? And a lot of mothers now work unsociable hours. They don't work nine to five any more. It's society isn't it?
>
> (Young mother in Bell *et al.* 2004: 38)

Quality is also a concern for many parents especially as their choice can be limited because of shortage of supply. In their annual survey of childcare costs the Day Care Trust (2005) found that 65 per cent of Children's Information Services reported that parents in their areas complained of a lack of available, affordable childcare.

The *Ten Year Strategy for Childcare*, published in December 2004 (HM Treasury, DfES, DWP, DTI 2004) aims to deliver childcare which meets the needs of parents to go out to work and it will be underpinned by a Childcare Act placing a duty on local authorities to ensure that there is 'sufficient' childcare in their areas. This policy was challenged in the press in October 2005, following the publication of new research into the type of childcare provision which is best for babies. The *Families, Children, and Childcare Project* by Penelope Leach, Kathy Sylva and Alan Stein (Oxford University Department of Educational Studies 2005) shows that one-to-one forms of care are best for babies under 18 months, recommending the care of childminders, nannies or, indeed, parents. Although the media tried to construct this as an argument against mothers of young children going out to work, in fact the authors were anxious to explain that it was no such thing; it simply indicated which forms of out-of-home care might be best for children of different ages. What is clear, however, is that very young children need consistent, nurturing relationships with a small number of adults in order to achieve optimal development and attachment relationships. These findings are entirely consistent with the work of all major child development theorists and practitioners since Bowlby's influential World Health Organization monograph in 1951 and in the practical work of Magda Gerber with very young children, their parents and their carers.

Children in need

In relation to assessments of vulnerable children, first in the *Framework for the Assessment of Children in Need and their Families* (DoH 2000), and currently in the CAF (DfES 2005b), to be implemented between April 2005 and the end of 2008, professionals are directed to assess the adequacy of parents with reference to identified tasks and attributes. For example, the current version of the CAF directs professionals to assess the quality of parenting by reference to a checklist covering matters such as whether or not the parent provides adequate practical care or abuses drugs or alcohol. Indicators of emotional warmth and stability are listed as being such things as parental feelings for the child, physical contact and frequency of house moves. In an attempt to standardize good practice, legislation and health and welfare policies have increasingly defined and detailed professional practice since the Children Act 1989. As can be seen in the CAF, professionals are now presented with a plethora of areas of judgement that can be viewed from a static and situational perspective. Although emphasis is placed, in guidance, on approaching assessments holistically, and not mechanistically, the manner in which CAF is presented, it can be argued, will lead professionals to concentrate on form rather than content. A snapshot in time may not reveal the actuality of life for a child, for good or ill, and there is real danger in presenting correlations between certain variables and child harm as causalities. For example, there may well be a correlation between substance abuse and child abuse but that does not mean that all parents with a drug dependency are poor parents. On the other hand, some children may be 'assessed' by many professionals over lengthy periods of time without their sufferings being recognized, as with Victoria Climbié (Laming 2003).

The CAF makes no mention as to how judgements are to be made. Policies lay great emphasis on the importance of multi-agency work to ensure that the varied knowledge bases and skills of the many professionals involved will come together positively and effectively for the benefit of the child. Attention, therefore, is placed on how the professional adults involved communicate with one another, not how professional adults can attune themselves to the world of the child through skilled, knowledge-based observation. An earlier publication issued by the DoH warns against the seductive appeal of positivist approaches to these complex issues:

> despite increasing sophistication in the design and evaluation of risk assessment tools, the variables for assessing children in the contexts of their families are so complex that professional judgement underpinned by theory and research still remains the cornerstone of best practice.
>
> (DoH 2001: 12)

The central importance of the relationship, between parent and child and the parent and professional must not be overlooked.

The Gerber approach to parent education

> the basic thing is that you have to respect and trust a ... baby's inborn capacities. His natural desire to take in from the world, to learn and take in, is very important. Anything that you would intrude into that would just disturb the natural flow. Our role is to create an environment in which the child can best do all the things that the child would do naturally. The misleading thing about this is that it sounds so easy. Most parents would say, 'Sure, that's what I want. Of course, that's what I want.' ... If you follow that now in this country, it's fully against what the whole society is all about ... The whole society pushes you constantly. In education what was expected at age seven in second grade is now done in nursery school. While what Emmi [Pikler] really stands for seems the simplest, the most natural thing to do. You don't have to do more. She doesn't say work more. She says work less. Enjoy more. Work less. Just sit and enjoy your child. It's a miracle. It does happen in front of your eyes. Yes, of course you have to be sensitive to your child's needs ... The child has to feel your caring presence. But, you don't have to teach. You don't have to buy more gadgets. You don't have to do anything. Both of you can just exist and enjoy the developing relationship between you.
>
> (Quoted in Petrie and Owen 2005: 37–8)

The late Dr Emmi Pikler founded the 'Loczy' Institute in Budapest, Hungary in 1946 at the request of the government to care for 60 infants up to 3 years. She had few resources and the child to carer ratio was high – a minimum of eight infants to one nurse. Pikler was a paediatrician and her child-centred approach, recognizing the competencies of very young children, was highly unusual for the time. She was also a scientist and compiled extensive records, including film, of the children's development. Loczy continues today under the directorship of her daughter, Anna Tardos, and there is persuasive evidence to show that children raised at Loczy in a residential setting develop optimally and are able to make healthy attachment relationships (David and Appell 2001). Her friend and colleague, Magda Gerber, took these ideas to the USA in the 1950s and used them in parent-infant education classes and daycare settings. She founded, together with her colleague Tom Forrest MD, Resources for Infant Educarers (RIE) in Los Angeles, a not-for-profit organization to promote 'educare' – a term she coined to convey the notion that learning and caring for infants were not separate activities. The Pikler/Gerber theory and practice of 'respectful' care for young children, developed since 1946 in vastly different countries, aims to support the competencies of young children and enable their carers (parents or care providers), to understand the cues of each individual child. Furthermore, a shared understanding of each child and common practices between parents and providers supports continuity of care and minimal disruption for young children in out-of-family care. The work of Pikler and Gerber has been considered in detail elsewhere (Petrie and Owen 2005) but here we will outline Gerber's approach to parent education.

Sometimes parent-infant education in the UK is based on giving parents information about the 'generic' baby. Perhaps their own children are cared for elsewhere in a crèche enabling parents to get together to support one another, share common problems and get appropriate help and advice about developmental milestones and ways of handling issues such as teething, sleeping, toileting and feeding. For those motivated to read there are a multitude of manuals aimed at parents offering similar advice. Even the media, with programmes such as *Supernanny*, aim to help parents survive the demands of their young children. In effect the problems presented by children to their parents or carers are the priority. The focus is on their demands and deficits rather than their competencies. The 'Gerber approach' to parent-infant education is somewhat different. She recommends a small group of infants and parents meeting weekly from as early as 6 weeks old for perhaps the first two years of a child's life. Through the classes parents are shown how to observe their children, who are first placed on a suitable carpeted area with parents sitting quietly behind their own child. As the children become more mobile they are presented with a larger, more challenging environment. A facilitator seated with the children comments quietly on the cues given by each child. Parents are encouraged to notice what their child can do for themselves from the earliest weeks. How they teach themselves and learn from their mistakes. How they begin to make relationships with others. Of perhaps greatest importance is when and how adults should intervene and when not to. After a period of observation parents are then able to reflect on their observations of their own child and the interactions between their child and other children – barely noticeable in the early weeks but of greater prominence as the children develop as social actors. In this way, parents are enabled to become fascinated by their child, to recognize and understand child development in practice and to be able to respond appropriately and thoughtfully. This process works also for childcare practitioners and has been found to be especially beneficial with young or untrained staff whose interest and involvement needs to be captured before they can become 'reflective practitioners'.

The environment is critical but can range from a small living-room to a corner of a large meeting hall. The important thing is that the environment is 'safe'. Safe, however, does not mean eliminating age-appropriate challenges and the opportunity to learn from making mistakes. Children should be able, for instance, to fall without hurting themselves, and adults shouldn't rush to pick them up, but wait to see if the child can recover from this by themselves and without fuss. Another consequence of this is that Gerber recommends children be kept in developmentally similar groups, even if their chronological age is different, as when children with some learning or physical impairments are part of the group. Pikler and Gerber observed over many decades that placing infants and toddlers together is satisfactory for neither age group as their learning needs are different and require different environments. If, as in families for example, both ages share the same environment, they recommend playpens of the old-fashioned wooden kind which enables a suitable infant environment to be created within the home. This advice is somewhat different to advice typically given to parents or childminders and flies in the face of current practice wisdom. Gerber is particularly insistent that infants and toddlers should not be overstimulated and 'toys' be very simple. In the earliest months a strong cotton square and perhaps a plastic cup and ball are the only objects made available to the child outside their own bodies. Unfettered gross motor development is an important aspect of the practices of both Pikler and Gerber and is seen as the key tool for learning which the child uses to understand themselves in relation to their environment and others. Magda Gerber also points out that to a very young baby their own fingers and hands are the best mobile. The infant begins to develop fine motor control – important 'work' for a young child. More detail about how parent-infant classes are run and the characteristics of suitable environments are presented by RIE practitioners in a recent book (Memel and Fernandez 2005). The following observation of a young child aged 9 months undertaken by a RIE practitioner, however, shows very clearly the competency of young children recognized by Pikler, Gerber and others:

> A nine month old in a RIE class in Silverlake, California, was observed playing with contented concentration for nineteen minutes with a cotton scarf. He did everything you could think of with that cloth: shook it, squeezed it, flipped it, transferred it from hand to hand, pushed it, pulled it, put it on his foot, hand, head, in his mouth, rubbed himself with it, threw it away and fetched it back, scrubbed the floor and wall with it, sat on it, lay down on it, played peek-a-boo with it. The scarf is truly an active player toy with endless possibilities.
>
> (Memel and Fernandez 2005: 98)

Pikler and Gerber demonstrated how to recognize the competences of the youngest infant, to understand their cues and therefore their needs more accurately. They have shown it is possible to give respect and choice to pre-verbal babies. Gerber developed ways of helping parents, which have since been utilized by RIE practitioners to support people from many different cultures, race heritages and socioeconomic circumstances, to observe and reflect on their own child's uniqueness and understand their non-verbal cues. This way of understanding and interacting with young children does not require expensive equipment or special environments. Not only is it an approach of benefit to parents but it is an approach that transfers easily to any type of out-of-family care. Systematic development of these principles and practices, with parents and childcare staff in all settings, would meet our current interest in providing services which are holistic and integrated, which recognize and provide for children's individual needs and which allow for the active participation of even the youngest child. Because the observations and reflections take place in a group of children, they also address some of the recent observations that western traditions of childcare practice are very focused on individual children at the expense of their membership in groups (Modigliani 2003).

Birth to Three Matters

In 2002 Gillian Pugh, the British early years' specialist, introduced a recent book on the care of babies with the following words:

> In the five years since the study was completed there has been very considerable change in government policy and in levels of provision for children under three, and also in our understanding of the

importance of the first three years of life. We now know from research, for example, how quickly the brain is developing during the first twelve months of life, and how susceptible it is to environmental influences. We also know that environmental stress has a negative effect not only on how the brain develops but also on how it functions, and this underlies our capacity to make and sustain relationships

(Edwards 2002: Introduction)

She referred to a period which did, indeed, see an unprecedented interest in the care and education that is provided for our youngest children, both by their own families and by others and, since 2002, even more developments have taken place in policy and strategy towards children's services. The Ten Year Childcare Strategy (HM Treasury 2004) can be seen as an attempt to rationalize, redesign and re-badge many of the previous initiatives into a more coherent policy which relates to the government's overall aims for children's services as outlined in the *Every Child Matters* policies beginning with the Green Paper of 2003. These developments give a much more prominent role than has previously been seen in childcare and education to the wishes and needs of parents and to a consultation process with children. Both of these are facilitated by the approaches to practice advocated by Gerber and by the *Birth to Three Matters* framework, though there are clearly differences: philosophical, cultural and to some degree, temporal.

In the past, children below the age of 3 have sometimes been a neglected age group, thought to be in daycare only because their parents worked rather than because the children could derive any positive benefit from the experience. The good baby was the quiet baby and activities revolved around keeping the child clean, fed, safe and rested. Little thought was given to ensuring that the parental and out-of-family care was congruent and based on the unique needs of each child rather than the needs of the adult carers. There have been, however, a number of pioneers in British early childhood education who have argued for a more sophisticated approach to work with the under-3s. Elinor Goldschmied, for instance, has written and taught for over 40 years, encouraging parents and carers to allow these youngest children to control the pace and nature of their own learning. The most widely known aspect of Goldschmied's work is the 'Treasure Basket' (Goldschmied and Jackson 2004). Goldschmied shares with Magda Gerber a stress on the importance of observing the rapidly developing baby and allowing them to dictate the pace and subject of their learning rather than having this imposed by adults. And it is this recognition of the capacity for learning of the youngest children and the relationship-based approach to meeting their learning needs which is reflected in most of the other national materials which have been produced in recent years, most notably *Birth to Three*

Matters. Professor Lesley Abbott undertook extensive consultation with the early years' sector and the conclusions drawn are remarkably similar to those identified by Pikler and Gerber (Petrie and Owen 2005). The central role of observation in determining the abilities and needs of individual children is critical. The role of caring adults is also important, in particular knowing when to intervene to support children's learning, as well as when *not* to intervene so that children can work things out for themselves or with other children. A quotation from the framework's introductory booklet gives an indication of the ethos:

> Babies and young children need support as they begin a journey of self-discovery from a base of loving and secure relationships with parents and/or a key person. The beginnings of autonomy can be seen in the relationships which exist as babies and young children play and explore alongside a close, attentive, warm and sensitive adult
>
> (DfES 2002: 8)

The principles and practices of caring for young children developed by Magda Gerber and inherent in her approach to parent education requires this degree of commitment and understanding but do not require expensive equipment or fancy environments.

Those offering 'education' to parents must be interested in children, as well as adults, and be prepared to sit quietly, observing, reflecting and learning, and modelling that behaviour to others. This may seem alien in a culture where we feel we have to keep children busy and are not being 'good' parents unless we fill their days with activity and their surroundings with colour and noise. Pikler and Gerber, through their own observations of children and child-centred practice, developed an integrated and holistic approach to all the environments in a child's life: home, daycare, parent support group and so on as a way of meeting the needs of children in a range of very different, sometimes challenging, situations. It is in this aspect of their work that the true value lies for children's services in the UK today. It offers the possibility of an approach which makes sense in any service, in any community, for children and for adults. Furthermore, the principles can make sense to professionals trained in any of the disciplines which are now being exhorted to work together to integrate their practice. If, to borrow the government's phrase, we are truly concerned to ensure that 'every child matters' then the potential for developing the work of Pikler and Gerber in the UK should be explored.

Conclusion

In spite of the rhetoric found in policies, services are rarely child-centred. Policies often fail to support a benign parent-child relationship and there seems to be an increasing emphasis on punishments for parents whose children behave in ways considered unacceptable. Such approaches increase tensions between adults and children. There has also been much evidence in recent years that flagship policies have failed to provide protection for children, such as Victoria Climbié, and optimal development opportunities for our youngest and most vulnerable children. New and proposed policies are unlikely to improve the situation for children significantly since, as argued earlier, they are primarily aimed at professional activity, structures and organizations rather than at supporting changes in our perception and understanding of children, particularly children under 3. All parents and carers can benefit from the confidence which comes from knowing their baby well and developing a respectful relationship with them as promoted by Gerber: a relationship based on recognizing what the baby can do and supporting them to meet new challenges in their own way. It is the most vulnerable children, however, entitled to family support services in the community including parent education, who could benefit most from Gerber's approach; an approach that promotes a particular kind of relationship between child and parent or carer and is time-rich but resource modest.

References

BBC News (2005a) Bad parents should be punished, 29 July, news.bbc.uk/1/hi/education/4727065.stm.

BBC News (2005b) Parents blamed for unruly pupils, 10 October, news.bbc.uk/go/pr/-/1/hi/education/4327670.stm.

Bell, J., Clisby, S., Craig, G., Measor, L., Petrie, S. and Stanley, N. (2004) *Living on the Edge: Sexual Behaviour and Young Parenthood in Rural and Seaside Areas*, Teenage Pregnancy Research Programme research briefing. London: TPU/DoH.

Bowlby, J. (1951) *Maternal Care and Mental Health*. Geneva: World Health Organization.

David, M. and Appell, G. (2001) *Loczy: An Unusual Approach to Mothering*. Hungary: Association Pikler-Loczy for Young Children.

Day Care Trust (2005) Parents pay Inflation-busting cost of childcare (press release), www.daycaretrust.org.uk.

DfES (2002) *Birth to Three Matters*. London: DfES Publications.

DfES (2005a) *Every Child Matters: Parents, Carers and Families*, www.everychild matters.gov.uk/parents/.
DfES (2005b) *Every Child Matters: Common Assessment Framework*, www.everychild matters.gov.uk/caf/.
DoH (2000) *Framework for the Assessment of Children in Need and their Families.* London: The Stationery Office.
DoH (2001) *Studies Informing the Framework for the Assessment of Children in Need and their Families.* London: TSO.
Edwards, A.G. (2002) *Relationships and Learning: Caring for Children from Birth to Three.* London: National Children's Bureau.
Goldschmied, E. and Jackson, S. (2004) People Under 3: Young Children in Day Care, 2nd edn. London: Routledge.
HM Treasury (2004) *Every Child Matters.* Norwich: TSO.
HM Treasury, DfES, DWP, DTI (2004) *Choice for Parents, the Best Start for Children: a Ten Year Strategy for Childcare.* London: HM Treasury.
Laming (2003) *The Victoria Climbié Inquiry: Report of an Inquiry by Lord Laming*, www.victoria-climbie-inquiry.org.uk/finreport/finreport.htm.
Memel, E. and Fernandez, L. (2005) RIE parent-infant guidance classes, in S. Petrie and S. Owen (eds) *Authentic Relationships in Group Care for Infants and Toddlers – Resources for Infant Educarers, Principles into Practice.* London: Jessica Kingsley.
Modigliani, K. (2003) 'Who says what is quality?' Setting childcare standards with respect for cultural differences, in A. Mooney and J. Statham (eds) *Family Day Care: International Perspectives on Policy, Practice and Quality.* London: Jesssica Kingsley.
Oxford University Department of Educational Studies (2005) *Families Children and Child Care Project*, www.edstud.ox.ac.uk/research/fell.html.
Petrie, S. and Owen, S. (2005) *Authentic Relationships in Group Care for Infants and Toddlers – Resources for Infant Educarers, Principles into Practice.* London: Jessica Kingsley.
Social Exclusion Unit (2005) *Breaking the Cycle: Taking Stock of Progress and Priorities for the Future.* London: SEU, www.socialexclusionunit.gov.uk.

12 Young Parents Matter

John Powell and Alison Lockley

This chapter explores the difficulties that many young parents face in raising their children in the UK. Young parents are often among the most disadvantaged and socially excluded of parents. Evidence indicates that young people who have aspirations for further or higher education, or prospects of career opportunities, don't opt for parenthood. Teenage parenthood, therefore, is often a scenario in which choice has not played a significant role and is, in fact, frequently a simple continuation of, and compliance with, accepted and expected family and community cultural patterns (Lockley 2001: 71).

Young parents have been the subject of much deliberation, research and intervention over the past five years or so. This attention has largely come about as a response to statistics which identified the UK as the country having the highest young teenage birth rate in western Europe, and third only to the USA and New Zealand in the developed world. New Labour identified young motherhood as one of a number of factors associated with social exclusion and their response to these statistics was to commission, in 1999, a report by the Social Exclusion Unit, *Teenage Pregnancy*, (TSO 1999) which identified and analysed causative links between the two issues. The findings of this report confirmed some of the indicators of social exclusion, such as experience of poverty, a history of being in care, being the daughter of a teenage mother, educational problems and truancy, lack of opportunities/participation post-school, a history of sexual abuse during childhood or adolescence and mental health problems to be among the common precursors to teenage pregnancy, and teenage parenthood was identified, in turn, as perpetuating existent social exclusion. As a consequence of this report the government established the Teenage Pregnancy Unit (TPU), originally placed within the auspices of the Department for Education and Skills (DfES) and now located in the Department of Health (DoH), which is charged with the task of developing and driving forward a national campaign to reduce the number of teenage conceptions. The campaign has had some success in reducing the numbers of young parents but evidence is showing that the impact of the work of the TPU is most notably evident among older teenagers and predominantly those who are still engaged with education and who have aspirations for further and higher education. Therefore, one consequence of the campaign to reduce teenage pregnancy is that the group of young people most likely to continue to become young parents are those who are disengaged from education and support agencies, such as Connexions, and who lack work and career opportunities. In other words, young parents continue to be over-represented among the most socially excluded of young people.

The government concern is to attempt to deal with issues of social exclusion through policies that recognize the needs of both young parents and their babies and young child(ren). In order to meet this concern, there have been a number of policies developed to inform practice that emanate from within the *Every Child Matters: Change for Children* programme (DfES 2004), including the Common Assessment Framework (CAF) which aims to ensure that every child receives the universal services to which they are entitled and any additional services they need at the earliest opportunity.

The CAF provides practitioners with a tool for identifying children who may have unmet needs through discussion with the child, their family and other appropriate practitioners. Through this process information may be gathered and a plan of action formulated for further involvement. In this context the child is also a parent attempting to deal with the difficulties of new parenthood and requiring a great deal of support to do so. The government has also identified that young parents and their children are a priority and appropriate support networks have been established for them through the *Every Child Matters* programme. At the centre of the programme is the focus on the community as the appropriate available resource for a diverse number of vulnerable groups including young parents. Through attendance at the community Sure Start centre the young parents' feelings of isolation that can reinforce their sense of exclusion can be addressed. As a means of further coordinating the needs of young parents, Sure Start Plus 'teams' were constructed to develop expertise:

> from across sectors, providing effective joined up working with local agencies and services, and enabl[ing] easier access to support for young pregnant women and young parents. These teams worked best when they provided both the generic support role of the adviser and [were] linked to specialist aspects of support such as: breastfeeding, smoking cessation, pregnancy options, re-integration to school and work with young fathers.
>
> (Wiggins *et al.* 2005:2)

This multi-agency approach to supporting young parents clearly suggests the importance of the need for coordinators to act as a link between the young parent and other appropriate agencies, putting the young person at the fore of agency involvement.

However, under New Labour it can be argued that social inclusion has been used not only to reinforce the labour market, but also to enforce a notion of social cohesion. Those who continue to exist outside the prescribed social boundaries are seen as potentially jeopardizing the cohesion and co-herence of society (Lockley and Powell 2002).

For New Labour, social inclusion is viewed as an aspect of social cohesion rather than of economic and social equality. Approaches to facilitate this form of 'inclusion' bring together labour market re-entry and a rejection of de-pendency on state benefits, along with policies to control the behaviour of those seen to threaten social cohesion (Burden and Hamm 2000: 191). Another reading of the policy support to young parents may be to view it as obliging the inclusion of certain groups and pressurizing them to do so. An example of this is the New Deal, whereby claimants must either participate or lose their benefit payments (Burden and Hamm 2000). The rationale may be that young parents can be seen to threaten social cohesion by virtue of their youth and their poverty. In addition, Levitas (1998) has suggested that the New Labour social exclusion agenda incorporates a concept of the poor as a 'moral underclass' who are culturally and morally different from the majority. Within this discourse, disadvantaged young people are stigmatized by the included majority as 'idle, criminal young men and single mothers' (1998: 9–21). Once again, this links to McRobbie's (1991) description of a crumbling and marginalized community.

Given these arguments, the recommendations of the SEU on teenage pregnancy could be perceived as enforcing, rather than enabling, the return of young parents to education and therefore employment. However, this is in line with the concerns mentioned earlier that Britain had the 'highest rates of teenage pregnancies in Europe and [that] the government committed itself to halving the numbers of pregnancies to under eighteen year olds by 2010' (Glennerster 2000: 225). The concept of social exclusion, therefore, offers an important framework within which the experiences of young parents can be better understood along with the part that the government plays in devel-oping inclusive strategies for them.

Social exclusion

The proximity of social exclusion to young parenthood raises certain conflicts for practitioners working with young parents. On the one hand there is the need to recognize young parenthood as a positive choice which, with ap-propriate support, can achieve an entirely satisfactory outcome for both parent and child, but on the other there is the reality that early parenthood is associated with a number of indicators of long-term and ongoing dis-advantage and exclusion.

The evidence gathered by the SEU report (1999: 26) indicates that young parents, in relation to older parents:

• are much more likely to have no qualifications by the age of 33;

- are more likely to be in receipt of means-tested benefits by the age of 33;
- if they are working … are more likely, in their twenties, to be working in unskilled or semi-skilled occupations;
- have a 20% chance of having four or more children by the age of 33 (if they are married or subsequently marry) … are more likely to be divorced or separated by their thirties …

It is also important to acknowledge that young parenthood is a predominantly female affair. Relationships often break down before the birth of the child and young partners often find the maintenance of shared care difficult to negotiate. Young fathers do exist, and can be supportive, and the practitioner can do much to promote the role of the father and thereby promote and normalize the idea of a shared-care relationship, but it is a fact that many young parents will be lone mothers and it may be useful, therefore, to highlight the level of disadvantage which can affect these families.

In 2003 Kiernan and Smith analysed statistics from the Millennium Cohort Study for the Office of National Statistics' Population Trends series. They looked at births outside marriage not only because of the increased numbers, from 6 per cent in the 1960s to 40 per cent in 2001, but specifically because 'there is accruing evidence, at least for Britain … that children born … to mothers not in a partnership … have less advantaged lives than their contemporaries who are born to married parents' (2003: 26). The Millennium Cohort Study looked at children, among others, who were living in the poorest wards based on the US Department of Education (DoE) weighted data for the UK Child Poverty Index, and found that 'non   co-residential parenthood is more common amongst those who live in   disadvantaged wards

Table 12.1 Level of household income and whether in receipt of income support, in context of partnership context at time of child's birth (weighted data for the UK; totals may not add up to 100 per cent due to rounding)

Household income	Very low	Low	Intermediate	High	Income support	No income support
Partnership context at birth						
Married	7.8	30.9	27.8	33.5	3.2	96.8
Cohabiting	21.0	40.7	20.9	17.4	12.7	87.4
Non-partnered	76.4	18.8	3.1	1.7	69.8	30.2
No. in sample	4,686	5,615	3,310	3,260	3,700	14,775

Source: Kiernan and Smith (2003: 30)

and in wards with high representations of the ethnic populations' (2003: 28). Table 12.1 shows the economic position of lone mothered families in the UK, according to Kiernan and Smith. These statistics clearly indicate that lone mothers, including young mothers, are likely to be on a very low income or dependent upon Income Support, which evidences the levels of poverty experienced by these families.

Research conducted by the Department of Health (DoH) indicates that young parents are also more likely to have experienced poverty themselves as a child and that the risk of becoming a young mother is almost ten times higher for a young woman whose family is in social class 'v' (unskilled manual) than those in social class 'i' (professional) (DoH 2003).

Young parents and their children

Having established that young parents may well be experiencing multiple disadvantages it is important to explore how these issues might impact upon their ability to parent their children. In a study conducted by Bloomfield *et al.*, young parents identified that everyone had an opinion about their abilities to parent:

> You know, everyone's got their little say, even complete strangers when you're shopping – 'Oh, I think he needs a bottle' – that's the challenge for me, other people's – what other people are saying to me, the pressures that they put on you, especially in-laws.
>
> (2005: 50)

In addition to everyone having a view about the level of care of their child, young parents felt that they were always being expected to be 'perfect':

> There is so much pressure on us as parents to be the perfect parent, to be seen to be bringing up perfect children, to run a nice home and to be the perfect wife, the list is endless on the pressures, I think, well, that is how I feel on being a parent, and sometimes I just feel I can't do this, I can't be perfect.
>
> (2005: 50)

It seems from this research that the expectation held by society is that most young parents are likely to need constant guidance and advice but that this is likely to be interpreted by the young parent as setting goals that are extremely difficult if not impossible to achieve and that they are therefore always likely to be considered as inadequate parents.

Another finding was that young parents were taken by surprise by the experience of becoming a parent and the demands of the role: 'Nothing prepared me, it was a total shock; I just couldn't believe how much life had changed' (Bloomfield *et al.* 2005: 51).

The difficulties that young parents experienced were concerned with setting, maintaining and being consistent regarding boundaries and dealing adequately with behaviour issues, discipline and handling conflicts, particularly at meal- and bedtimes. Issues were also identified relating to communicating with their child, including understanding their moods, and listening and responding appropriately. They also expressed concerns that they themselves didn't feel that they knew what was appropriate regarding their knowledge of child development: feelings of failure. Being consistent in responding to their child's demands was clearly problematic.

In addition to these issues Heaven (1994) raises the concern that 'teenage mothers have been observed to provide less stimulation to their children'. He goes on to argue that 'teenage mothers have unrealistic expectations about developmental milestones' (p. 160). Although this is an earlier piece of research to that of Bloomfield *et al.* there are some clear resonances between them. Heaven also suggests that young parents are more likely to be 'punitive' towards their child, which relates to the issues identified by Bloomfield *et al.* regarding discipline and boundaries. However, Bloomfield is attempting to identify what young parents perceive as issues in order to develop a supportive response to them through their participation in effective parenting programmes.

Young parents and available services

It is of course important for young parents to be able to access their Sure Start children's centre and through this to be referred to other practitioners representing a multi-agency infrastructure, some of whom are likely to become involved in assessing the needs of a young parent so that the young parent can be referred to an effective parenting programme. In this regard a key service for teenage parents is the Sure Start Plus pilot which developed from the action plan of the teenage pregnancy report published by the SEU in 1999:

> This report highlighted the increased risks of poor health and social outcomes faced by teenage parents and their children, including a 60% higher rate of infant mortality; 25% increased risk of low birth weight babies; and three times the rate of postnatal depression. In addition, teenage mothers were reported to have low educational attainment. Sure Start Plus was developed to reduce the risk of long-term social exclusion associated with teenage pregnancy by 'providing intensive support for parents and child to help them with housing, health care, parenting skills, education and child care'.
>
> (Wiggins *et al.* 2005)

Sure Start Plus operates as a multi-agency support network in galvanizing professional support to meet the needs of the young parent and her child. In addition it also links to other appropriate programmes such as *Every Child Matters* which similarly is concerned with activating professional intervention as the central response to the needs of the child. The programme is able to access educational partners as well as others representing health and social care but the immediate involvement is to assess the needs of the young parent, and her needs, in this case, are in relation to her baby. *Every Child Matters: Change for Children* (DfES 2004) has developed an outcomes framework for practitioners to measure their input against, and subsequently allow them to be more able to meet the needs of, children and young people. The degree to which practitioners agree about the needs of a mother and child will tend to vary and is often linked to practitioner status and whose voice carries the most weight (Powell 2005). However, the five outcomes which are introduced through *Every Child Matters: Change for Children* with their focus on health, staying safe, enjoyment and achievement, making a positive contribution and achieving economic well-being offer the opportunity for a clearer rationale regarding practitioner involvement. There are still possible tensions between the perspectives of practitioners and those held by young parents, particularly regarding views of what is appropriate and what is acceptable. It may well be the case that a nursery or a childminder are viewed as fit for the purpose of caring for the young parent's child but this may not match the view of the young parent.

The issue of accessible childcare is significant for young parents and it has been found that they frequently demonstrate a preference for private nursery childcare, as it is apparent that young mothers, in particular, are anxious about being supplanted in their child's affections by a childminder who could be perceived as a competing mother figure (Lockley and Powell 2002). However, private nursery care is probably that which is least accessible for young parents, both in terms of a lack of finances to fund the care, and, additionally, in the levels of self-confidence required to locate and approach a private nursery establishment. The government has recently initiated a funding scheme, 'Care to Learn?' which makes childcare costs payable to young parents in education or training. Although this is accepted as being a generous benefit, and has greatly eased young parents' ability to access paid childcare, it is still not sufficient to finance full-time private nursery education. It will, however, fund a childminder for the hours parents require to attend most further education courses and, given that childminders can often be accessed via more informal routes, this is often the childcare that young parents actually gravitate towards. This means that the professional early years practitioner may not actually come into contact with many young parents, unless they are working in a local authority establishment which provides subsidized or free places to less advantaged families, or there are

difficulties expressed about the young parent's ability to look af
It is in the childcare placement where they take their own child u..
young parent may come in contact with the *Birth to Three Matters* framework
(DfES 2002) to support children. There are remarkable similarities between
the five outcomes identified in *Every Child Matters* and those in the *Birth to
Three Matters* framework with its focus on four main aspects of the child
which emphasize ways of understanding 'effectiveness' in the following ways:
having a consistent carer both at home and in the childcare setting; recognizing that babies and young children are competent learners from birth;
and that learning is a shared process. The care of an adult is extremely important to the child's sense of well-being; children are able to be given appropriate responsibility and allowed to make mistakes because they learn
better by being actively involved. Finally children are vulnerable and their
independence relies on having someone there who is dependable. The
structure of the framework is also useful for young parents since it clearly
articulates the central aspects of the child that can be considered both with
the childcare provider and by parents themselves.

The young person as a parent

Apart from the previously discussed economic disadvantages, young parents
can be perceived as 'effective' parents or 'less effective' parents (see Bloomfield
et al. 2005) in the same way as those from any other age group. The authors
have worked with young mothers who have been consistently dedicated to
the care of their children and who have adopted a very considered approach
to their parenting responsibilities. However, as we have previously discussed,
the reality for today's young parents is that they are over-representative of
those young people who have already been disadvantaged by the obstacles
and barriers presented by factors of social exclusion. One of the outcomes of
this disadvantage can be a childhood which has lacked parental input from
their own parents and, unsurprisingly, this will frequently impact upon their
ability to understand and develop the many skills and behaviours required for
responsible parenthood. Additionally, although a level of *physical* maturity is
an obvious requirement for reproduction, *emotional maturity* is not such an
intrinsic characteristic. Levels of emotional maturity can be widely diverse in
a group of young parents of a similar chronological age. Some will clearly be
children with their own unfulfilled parenting needs and others will be responsible young adults with a mature approach to their own children's well-
being. However, most young parents will require some support, whether
practical or emotional, in order to cope with the unexpected and sometimes
unwelcome demands of a small infant.

Many young parents will be struggling with competing priorities. They are parents but they may not have completed their own education or established themselves in a social circle, or developed a relationship with a partner. These needs can make caring for a small and needy infant appear to be an over-whelming and unachievable task and will impact upon the parenting the child receives. In the consumerist times in which we currently live, young parents can be disproportionately affected by the pressure to conform to the images of fashion presented by the media. There can be a tendency to see the baby as a fashion accessory who must wear miniaturized versions of the latest styles. Sometimes, this desire to present a certain image can detract from the young mother's view of her child as an individual with emotional and physical needs.

The potential role of the practitioner

All of this means that the practitioner needs to have an awareness of the types of obstacles young parents may have experienced, and may continue to ex-perience, as they attempt to parent their children. A good understanding of the effects of long-term disadvantage, including that of living in poverty, lacking in parental guidance and even of being 'in care', is required by early childhood practitioners alongside the ability to provide support and guidance in a non-patronizing way. Young people often have only a tentative re-lationship with self-confidence and they will avoid perceived authority fig-ures who even unwittingly undermine that fragility. Young parents will often be subject to peer pressure in the same way as other young people and the early years practitioner will need to be sensitive to the fact that the young parent will be in older adolescence as well as being a mother or father.

The reality will be that many young mothers, in particular, will be very 'needy', and in these circumstances there can be a tendency to confuse a positive, supportive relationship with friendship. Therefore, care must be taken to ensure that the support offered does not encourage dependence; the intention should always be that the young parent develop the skills and confidence themselves to provide the care their child needs outside of the childcare situation.

Practitioners will be accustomed to the principle of stimulating the in-terest of the children they care for or educate. The same requirements will be present when working with young people; their interest needs to be engaged and their participation encouraged rather than advice being delivered as a lecture. Providing the opportunity for the young parent to have hands-on practice at certain tasks, from baby bottle sterilizing to providing stimulating play sessions, is as essential for young parents as much as for any other par-ents, since parents do not emerge with these skills, nor are they innate. The *Birth to Three Matters* framework can support this relationship by offering a joint focus that both the young parent and their childcare provider should find central to providing purpose to their relationship. The central paradigm for the framework would be to tap into the mutual interest held by the young parent and the care provider regarding the progress of the young child by considering them through the appropriate components of: a Strong Child; a Skilful Communicator; a Competent Learner and a Healthy Child. This approach combines the aims of Sure Start Plus and the five outcomes for well-being cited in *Every Child Matters*, and through the practices of supporting their children in the framework components the young parent should develop confidence to become more effective.

References

Bloomfield, L., Kendall, S., Applin, L., Attarzadeh, V., Dearnley, K., Edwards, L., Hinshelwood L, Lloyd P and Newcombe T (2005) A qualitative study exploring the experiences and views of mothers, health visitors and family support centre workers on the challenges and difficulties of parenting Health and Social Care in the Community 13(1), 46–55

Burden, T. and Hamm, T. (2000) Responding to socially excluded groups. Chapter 10 in Percy-Smith J. (Ed.) *Policy responses to social exclusion: towards inclusion?* Open University Press: Buckingham.

Burden T. and Hamm T. (2000) Responding to socially excluded groups, in J. Percy-Smith (ed.) *Policy Responses to Social Exclusion: Towards Inclusion?* Buckingham: Open University Press.

DfES (2002) *Birth to Three Matters*. London: DfES Publications.

DfES (2004) *Every Child Matters: Change for Children*. Nottingham: TSO.

DoH (2003) Health Minister sets out new phase of teenage pregnancy strategy, www.dh.gov.uk.

Glennester, H. (2000) *British Social Policy since 1945*, 2nd edn. Oxford: Blackwell.

Heaven, P. (1994) *Contemporary Adolescence: A Social Psychological Approach*. Melbourne: Macmillan.

Kiernan, K. and Smith, K. (2003) *Unmarried Parenthood: New Insights from the Millenium Cohort Study in Population Trends*, 144 (Winter 2003). London: ONS.

Levitas, R. (1998) *The Inclusive Society? Social Exclusion and New Labour*. London: Macmillan Press Ltd.

Lockley, A. (2001) With regard to young mothers are the government's welfare to work initiatives likely to be implementable or successful? Unpublished thesis, Manchester Metropolitan University.

Lockley, A. and Powell, J. (2002) *The Stockport Young Parents Project Interim Report* (unpublished).

McRobbie, A. (1991) *Feminism and Youth Culture: From* Jackie *to* Just Seventeen. London: Macmillan.

Powell, J. (2005) Multiprofessional perspectives, in L. Jones, R. Holmes and J.

Powell, *Early Childhood Studies; A Multiprofessional Perspective*. Maidenhead: Open University Press.

Social Exclusion Unit (SEU) (1999) *Teenage Pregnancy*. London: TSO.

Wiggins, M., Rosato, M., Austerberry, H., Sawtell, M. and Oliver, S. (2005) *Supporting Teenagers who are Pregnant or Parents. Sure Start Plus National Evaluation: Executive Summary*. www.ioe.ac.uk/ssru/reports/ssplusexecutivesummary2005.pdf.

13 Children and Parents Matter: Research Insights from Integrated Child and Family Services in Australia

Ann Farrell, Collette Tayler and Lee Tennent[1]

Early years research is replete with evidence of the benefits of high-quality early childhood care and education for children and their families (Barnett 1995; McCain and Mustard 1999; Feinstein 2003; Sylva *et al.* 2003). Policy initiatives such as Australia's National Agenda for Early Childhood (2004), in turn, draw on a corpus of early years research as a backdrop to support children and their families, to promote child-friendly communities and to engender engagement in such communities. Britain's *Birth to Three Matters* framework (DfES 2002) also draws on an early years research base to support young children as strong and competent learners and skilful communicators, who matter to those involved in early years contexts. *Birth to Three Matters* shares, with the research reported in this chapter, a conceptual understanding that parents and families are central to the well-being of the child and that children and parents matter in research-driven initiatives to integrate child and family services. This chapter provides evidence from research conducted by the authors in Queensland (Australia) that the perspectives of parents and children can and should matter in the development and provision of integrated child and family services. The chapter maps the provision of programmes and activities for parents within the research sites and concludes with strategies for supporting parents, as well as their children, in their everyday lives.

[1] The authors acknowledge and herald the fine contribution of their late colleague and team member, Associate Professor Carla Patterson of Queensland University of Technology. Carla passed away in 2005 and leaves an ongoing legacy through her published work and participation in the study that is reported in this chapter.

Researching child and family services

The authors lead a trans-disciplinary, cross-sectoral partnership in Queensland, researching the development and impact of integrated child and family services, known as 'hubs' (Farrell *et al.* 2002, 2003, 2004a; Tayler *et al.*, 2005a, 2005b; Tennent *et al.* 2005). Against a history of often disjointed services and within the spirit of Australia's Stronger Families Agenda (2000), the Queensland hubs were envisioned to provide integrated childcare and early years services where service provision has proved challenging (Bush *et al.* 2002). Integration has been championed by government as a means of improving cross-sectoral access to and delivery of services to families. Initiatives akin to the hubs are also seen in the UK's children's centres, which, as part of the Sure Start strategy, are designed to serve as integrated one-stop-shops for childcare, health, education, employment and parenting support (DfES 2004).

Similar to many integration initiatives in other parts of the world, the Queensland hub initiative is primarily directed at disadvantaged and/or rural or remote communities. However, a distinguishing feature of the Queensland hubs is that they are largely community-driven. Each hub has been funded in response to submissions developed by local individuals and/or community groups, often comprising a core of committed and community-minded parents. Common to all hubs was a requirement that they provide services offering support to parents and families. The precise nature of these services, though, was very much dependent on the perceived or expressed needs of community members. As a result, each of the hubs is unique to the community that it serves.

Support for parents

A deliberate focus of the hub initiative was support for parents. This focus was underscored by evidence linking children's health, social and educational problems to family relationships. Studies demonstrate that family risk factors including poor parenting, family conflict and marriage breakdown have a significant impact on children's development (Vimpani 2004). Particularly in neighbourhoods or communities where extended networks are breaking down, divorce rates are high, and single and blended families are common, parents more than ever need support in learning to cope (Sanders 1999).

While strengthening parenting undoubtedly has the potential to improve child health and quality of life, we argue that broadening or strengthening the personal support networks of both parents and children and improving the social environments in which they live hold the key. Indeed, extensive research from different parts of the world suggests that the quality of family support and networks and ready access to appropriate services and informa-tion can, and do, ameliorate many of the disadvantages of individual families (Duncan *et al.* 1998; Edgar 2002; Ford *et al.* 2003). Ironically, it is often those who are in the greatest need of additional, more consistent and responsive sources of support who are least likely to have access to them.

As researchers interested in the social contexts of family well-being, it is our view that the hub initiative has the potential to enhance family and community capacity by building sense of community and social capital. Sense of community, defined as the feeling of belonging in a group (Tennent *et al.* 2005), has been linked to gains in health and well-being (Prezza *et al.* 2001; Farrell *et al.* 2004b). Social capital or social relations and networks based on trust and reciprocity are similarly associated with family well-being, reduced crime and a range of other positive health and education outcomes (Teach-man *et al.* 1996; Baron *et al.* 2000; Baum *et al.* 2000; Lochner *et al.* 2003; Schuller *et al.* 2004). Empirical evidence from social epidemiological studies, for instance, reveals that high levels of social capital have a positive effect on mortality rates, self-reported health status, access to healthcare, normal de-velopment in at-risk children and children's quality of life (see e.g. Pan *et al.* 2005). Social capital is thought to influence health by increasing access to social support including emotional support and information, social influence on behaviour, engagement and attachment, and access to shared resources and material goods (Pan *et al.* 2005).

According to Jack (2004), there is evidence that the social networks of parents and the social capital of the community in which they live contribute to differences in rates of officially identified child abuse. Some studies have identified a tendency for higher levels of maltreatment to be associated with parents who are socially isolated, lacking support from relatives and friends, or who live in socially impoverished areas, characterized by low levels of trust, where there is a lack of integration between personal and community net-works (Higgins and McCabe 1998).

A recent study in the UK by Gill *et al.* (2000), for instance, found that parents living in socially impoverished areas, where social interactions at the community level were limited, were heavily dependent on close relatives living nearby for their social support. Those parents who lacked local supportive family networks were more likely to experience higher levels of personal stress, poor health and serious problems in caring for their children. What was alarming in the study, Jack (2004) noted, was that families rarely, if ever, mentioned welfare professionals or formal services as being sources of information and support.

While social isolation is, in itself, cause for concern, many people living in rural or remote communities also experience geographic isolation from relevant services due to their living some hundreds of kilometres from their nearest town or centre. It is also widely known that the health of Australians who live in rural or remote areas is worse on a range of indicators than that of

Australians who live in more populated areas (Patterson 2000). Rural Australians suffer higher mortality, morbidity and hospitalization rates due to disproportionately high rates of suicide, injury and certain illnesses such as diabetes. As Dixon and Welch (2000) note, living and working in rural communities, especially in the most remote parts of Australia, is a health hazard. In addition, sustained reduction in government funding to health, welfare and education has a deleterious effect on many services in rural areas. Not surprisingly, these cutbacks have serious consequences for those living in such areas, particularly women, 77 per cent of whom have been found to have no family living close by (Morda *et al.* 2000). Thus, for parents living in rural and remote regions, family support hubs can provide vital access to a range of supports and information that would otherwise be unavailable to them.

The current study

As a cross-sectorial, whole-of-government study, our research partnership comprises Australia's Commonwealth Department of Family and Community Services, Queensland's Department of Communities, Education Queensland, Queensland Health, Queensland's Commission for Children and Young People, the Crèche and Kindergarten Association of Queensland and researchers from the Centre for Learning Innovation, Queensland University of Technology (with funding from the Australian Research Council and research partners). We investigated 6 of the 19 hubs, with a focus on social capital, sense of community, health and well-being as children and adults engaged with the hubs and their services.

The research has a multi-phase, longitudinal, mixed-method design and uses interviews, surveys and focus group discussions to generate data. Participant groups include parents who are current or potential hub users, their children (aged 4–8 years), hub personnel and service providers within the hub community. In this chapter we outline the issue of support for parents in the light of our findings from parent surveys and focus group discussions with parents and service providers.

Services

To understand the scope and nature of the six hubs, we asked coordinators to list the various services, activities and programmes that were offered from their respective hubs. As can be seen in Table 13.1, all hubs offered information about, or referral to, a range of family support services. Each hub also offered one or more services or activities for children. Other supports and specific activities tended to be provided in response to perceived or expressed community need or according to the skills and abilities of the coordinator.

Table 13.1 Services and programmes offered by hubs

Parent-focused services/ programmes	Hub 1	Hub 2	Hub 3	Hub 4	Hub 5	Hub 6
Information about/ referral to services	x	x	x	x	x	x
Parenting programmes/ workshops	x	x	x	x		x
Individual counselling		x	x		x	x
Work/life skills programmes	x		x	x		x
Community directory/ newsletter	x	x	x		x	x
Resource library	x	x	x	x		x
Parent recreation activities (e.g. craft, yoga)		x	x	x		x
Financial/ transport assistance						x

Child-focused services/ programmes	Hub 1	Hub 2	Hub 3	Hub 4	Hub 5	Hub 6
Childcare/ childminding		x	x	x	x	x
Children's activities (e.g. holiday programmes, playgroup)	x	x	x	x	x	
Whole family and community activities	x	x				

In recognition of the important and often difficult task of parenting, most hubs offered a variety of programmes and activities to facilitate parenting (see Table 13.1). The availability of specific programmes across the hubs varied, but they included parent workshops and information sessions (such as Positive Parenting, Keeping Children Safe, Positive Parenting Program, ADHD, Getting Kids to Eat) and the facilitation of support groups (such as ADHD Parents, Parenting for Dads, Grandparents Support Group, Breastfeeding, Pram Walkers and Time out for Mums). In addition, some hubs provided programmes in professional and life skills such as computer training, work readiness, first aid, budgeting, as well as recreational activities such as fitness and craft.

Each hub offered one or more children's services or activities such as childcare, playgroup, holiday programmes, language and literacy activities, and visiting theatre groups. Two hubs also regularly organized whole family and community activities.

Parent awareness and usage of the hubs

Commendable as the hub initiative is, its potential is unlikely to be realized if services remain unknown or underutilized. We distributed questionnaires which asked parents and caregivers to indicate both their awareness and their usage of the hub facility. Overall, around two-thirds of families indicated that they were aware of their hub. However, awareness of the hubs varied widely across the communities with rates as high as 100 per cent in one community and as low as 47 per cent in another. Many, who were unaware of the hub or were unfamiliar with its services, commented that they would like to know more about the hub and what it offered. On average, less than half of the families in this study told us that they actually made use of the services on offer. Again, there was wide variation across the communities and it was apparent that awareness of a hub did not necessarily translate into usage. Given that the primary reason for lack of use may be lack of awareness of the services, it is imperative for hub designers and funding bodies to consider the awareness dimension in extending the reach of a hub.

Benefits of the hubs

In order to gauge the success and impact of each of the hubs, we asked parents to comment on the benefits of such services for themselves, their children and their community at large. Parents in all hub sites told us that they benefited from increased opportunities for socialization through hub activities and referrals, and the capacity to undertake work or study due to the availability of affordable childcare. Parents in most sites also expressed an appreciation of learning new skills acquired through hub programmes and having time out from children to attend appointments. Many parents also told us that their participation in hub programmes had led to improved parenting skills. Some examples of these comments were:

- learn about strategies and different ideas to handle situations;
- someone to understand my situation, discuss different techniques and know I'm not alone, there are people in the same situation;
- gives me strength and builds up more knowledge, understanding and coping skills;
- learning to control stress with naughty children;
- help with ideas for how to talk to my children about various stuff;
- triple P was great – many useful tips which helped to improve my relationship with my children;
- I was having attitude problems with one of my children and IMPS helped me see things in a different way which really helped;
- many families require assistance and information about raising children into thinking, responsible adults; also, parents require this service to build confidence in their parenting skills.

Parents also told us that their children benefited from their (parent) participation in parenting courses at the hub. As some parents stated:

- children benefit from newly-acquired parenting skills;
- happier because mum is happier;
- I am a happier, relaxed mum which helps them be more relaxed and happy;
- a happier, calmer mum.

According to parents, the hub also benefited the wider community. As one parent reported, 'the more support families have, especially when their children are young, the stronger the community will be'. Another stated that the hub had 'brought the community together'.

Impacts and issues relating to the hubs

Stakeholder focus group discussions held at each of the six hubs formed an integral part of data collection. These discussions not only provided an opportunity to further explore issues raised in the family and service provider questionnaires, they also enabled parents, service providers and the co-ordinator to get together. For some participants, this was their first visit to the hub. We asked each group several questions that focused on the potential and realized impacts of the hub, other supports that, with additional funding, could be provided from the hub, the skills and abilities required for an effective coordinator, and the consequences of the closure of the hub should funding cease.

A predominant theme to emerge was the importance and impact of networking and increased social and professional support. Discussions revealed that, for participants, heightened awareness of services had resulted in the growth of family social and support networks. This seemed to be of immense reassurance to many families. For those in lower-income areas, in particular, networks can help rebuild diminished social capital and contribute to positive relationships between parents and children. The availability of childcare services at a reduced cost was a recurring topic in all hub sites as it freed parents to re-enter the workforce or engage in further study or training.

For a majority of the hub sites, lack of transport remained an issue. Although it was beneficial to have a variety of services available from one location, many families mentioned that access to private transport was problematic and public transport to the hub was unavailable. Thus, a shuttle bus service was identified in some hubs as a priority should additional funding become available.

Discussions at all six hubs revealed that networking, counselling and flexibility were the skills most required for the role of hub coordinator. The groups believed that a hub coordinator is someone who needs to be out in the community sourcing services, determining which of these would be of benefit to the community and then raising awareness within the community of these services. Other skills such as counselling and marketing were also seen to be necessary.

The sustainability of programmes funded under fixed-term project initiatives remains a serious concern. So positive was the perceived impact of the hub on the community, that all groups expressed substantial concern about the impact on the community if the hub ceased to operate in the event that funding was withdrawn. There was widespread concern that the closure of the hubs would result in increased social isolation and decreased community sentiment, and exacerbate the already difficult circumstances faced by many families. As one parent commented, 'it's kind of like a lifeline'. While a service provider said that the vulnerable families within the community would 'probably just climb back into their shell and retract themselves because there is nowhere for them to go and no one for them to talk to'.

Conclusion

Our research confirms the centrality of parents and the ongoing need for support for parents within the context of family support hubs. Parent input into this research reinforced key principles which underpin the *Birth to Three Matters* framework, namely, that parents and families are central to the well-being of the child and that children's relationships with other people (including adults) are of crucial importance to them. A chief tenet of our research is that of listening to parents and to children throughout the planning, implementation and evaluation phases of the hub initiatives.

Evidence provided in this chapter indicates that parents value the opportunity to speak and be heard regarding issues which most affect them in their childrearing and community engagement. Furthermore, parents (as well as hub personnel) value the opportunity to contribute to service provision and its evaluation in their local area. Parent engagement, in turn, is central to developing authentic partnerships within communities, in order to promote and to optimize 'good beginnings' (Edgar 2002).

References

Barnett, S. (1995) Long term effects of early childhood programmes on cognitive and school outcomes, *The Future of Children*, 5(3): 25–50.

Baron, S., Field, J. and Schuller, T. (eds) (2000) *Social Capital: Critical Perspectives*. Oxford: Oxford University Press.

Baum, F., Palmer, C., Modra, C., Murray, C. and Bush, R. (2000) Families, social capital and health, in I. Winter (ed.) *Social Capital and Public Policy in Australia*. Melbourne: Australian Institute of Family Studies.

Bush, R., Johansson, A. and Finsterle, K. (2002) Community Engagement Benchmarks. Paper prepared for workshop on the nature of social capital and its implications for policy development, Brisbane, 3 July.

DfES (2002) *Birth to Three Matters*. London: DfES Publications.

DfES (2004) *Five Year Strategy for Children and Learners*. London: DfES Publications.

Department of Family and Community Services (2004) *The National Agenda for Early Childhood: A Draft Framework*, www.facs.gov.au/internet/fascinternet.ns/family/early_childhood.htm.

Dixon, J. and Welch, N. (2000) Researching the rural-metropolitan health differential using the social determinants of health, *Australian Journal of Rural Health*, 8: 254–60.

Duncan, G.J., Yeung, W., Brooks-Gunn, J. and Smith, J. R. (1998) How much does childhood poverty affect the life chances of children? *American Sociological Review*, 63: 406–23.

Edgar, D. (2002) Early childhood and the community. Keynote address for Early Childhood Matters Conference, Department of Human Services, Victoria Monash University, 5 October.

Farrell, A., Tayler, C. and Tennent, L. (2002) Early childhood services: what can children tell us? *Australian Journal of Early Childhood*, 27(3): 12–18.

Farrell, A., Tayler, C. and Tennent, L. (2003) Social capital and early childhood education, *Perspectives on Educational Leadership*, 13(7): 1–2.

Farrell, A., Tayler, C. and Tennent, L. (2004a) Building capital in early childhood education and care: an Australian study, *British Educational Research Journal*, 30(5): 623–32.

Farrell, S.J., Aubrey, T. and Coulombe, D. (2004b) Neighbourhoods and neighbours: do they contribute to personal well being? *Journal of Community Psychology*, 31(1): 9–25.

Feinstein, L. (2003) Inequality in early cognitive development of British children in the 1970 cohort, *Economica*, 7: 73–97.

Ford, R.M., Evans, D., Sine, J.P. and McDougall, S.J.P. (2003) Progressing in tandem: a sure start initiative for enhancing the role of parents in children's early education, *Educational and Child Psychology*, 20(4): 80–95.

Gill, O., Tanner, C. and Bland, L. (2000) *Family Support: Strengths and Pressures in a High Risk Neighbourhood*. Barkingsdale: Barnado's.

Higgins, D. and McCabe, M. (1998) The 'Child Maltreatment: Risk and Protection' model – evidence for a new approach to maltreatment research. Paper presented to 'Changing Families, Challenging Futures', 6th Australian Institute of Family Studies Conference, Melbourne 25–7 November.

Jack, G. (2004) Child protection at the community level, *Child Abuse Review*, 13: 368–83.

Lochner, K.A., Kawachi, I., Brennan, R.T. and Buka, S.L. (2003) Social capital and neighbourhood mortality rates in Chicago, *Social Science and Medicine*, 56: 1797–805.

McCain, M. and Mustard, F. (1999) *Reversing the Brain-drain: The Early Years Study*, final report, Children's Secretariat, http://www.childsec.gov.on.ca.

Morda, R., Kapsalakis, A. and Clyde, M. (2000) Reconceptualising child care in rural areas: meeting the needs? *Australian Journal of Early Childhood*, 25(2): 7–11.

Pan, R.J., Littlefield, D., Valladollid, S.G., Tapping, P.J. and West, D.C. (2005) Building healthier communities for children and families: applying asset-based community development to paediatrics, *Pediatrics*, 115(4): 1185–7.

Patterson, C. (2000) The emergence of rural health research in Australia, *Australian Journal of Rural Health*, 8: 280–5.

Prezza, M., Amici, M., Roberti, T. and Tedeschi, G. (2001) Sense of community referred to the whole town: its relations with neighbouring, loneliness, life satisfaction, and area of residence, *Journal of Community Psychology*, 29(1): 29–52.

Sanders, M.R. (1999) Effective family intervention: from clinical trials to public health, in M. Sawyer (ed.) *Rotary and Science in Australia: Evidence, Action and Partnership in Mental Health*. Parramatta, NSW: Australian Rotary Health Research Fund.

Schuller, T., Preston, J., Hammond, C., Brassett-Grundy, A. and Bynner, J. (2004)

The Benefits of Learning: The Impact of Education on Health, Family Life and Social Capital. London: Routledge.

Sylva, K., Melhuish, E., Sammons, P., Siraj-Blatchford, I., Taggart, B. and Elliott, K. (2003) *The Effective Provision of Pre-school Education (EPPE) Project: Findings from the Pre-school Period,* www.ioe.ac.uk/schools.ecpe/eppe/eppe/eppefindings.htm.

Tayler, C., Farrell, A., Tennent, L. and Patterson, C. (2004) *Child and Family Hubs and Social Capital: Issues Paper 3.* Brisbane: Commission for Children and Young People, Queensland Government.

Tayler, C., Farrell, A., Tennent, L. and Patterson, C. (2005a) Researching communities: towards beneficence, in A. Farrell (ed.) *Ethical Research with Children.* Maidenhead: Open University Press.

Tayler, C., Farrell, A., Tennent, L. and Patterson, C. (2005b) Researching social capital and community capacity in child and family hubs: insights for practitioner-researchers, policy makers and communities, *International Journal of Early Childhood Education,* 11(1): 139–53.

Teachman, J., Paasch, K. and Carver, K. (1996) Social capital and dropping out of school early, *Journal of Marriage and the Family,* 58(3): 773–83.

Tennent, L., Farrell, A., Tayler, C. and Patterson, C. (2005) *Social Capital and Sense of Community: What Do they Mean for Young Children's Success at School?* Australian Association for Educational Research, www.aare.edu.ac.uk.index. htm.TEN05115.

Vimpani, G. (2004) Refashioning child and family health services in response to family, social and political change, *Australian Health Review,* 27(2): 13–16.

14 Future Matters

Lesley Abbott

As we come to the end of a book which has celebrated the very special relationship between parent and child, it is tempting to merely draw the threads together and present a tidy picture of a future in which, if certain things are in place, all will be well. However, life is not like that and futures are uncertain, as Mark Vandevelde, a young student writing about information and communications technology (ICT) in a book to celebrate the millennium indicates:

> A cognitive chasm will separate anybody old enough to have contributed to this book from the children born into the new millennium. Because it is now possible to make tentative predictions about the developmental needs of children in the informational society, early childhood education can begin to redefine its role for social economic, cultural and political mutations which are now unfolding.
>
> (Vandevelde 2000: 125)

Gillian Pugh also writes about her vision for the future with specific reference to young children, families and communities. She takes the year 2010 when she envisages an early childhood centre for children aged from birth to 6 attached to a primary school:

> The centre was part of a flexible network of services for families with young children, next door to a health centre and providing a drop in facility for local childminders. There was a range of services for parents, including discussion groups about bringing up children and access to adult education classes and training opportunities and parents were fully involved in all aspects of their children's learning and in the centre's management.
>
> (Pugh 1999: 180)

In her role as chief executive of Coram Family she was able to realize this vision in the form of the Thomas Coram Children's Centre well before this date.

Each of the major documents published in recent years attests the present government's commitment to achieving this same vision and acknowledges the power and influence of parents on the development and learning of babies and young children. The ten-year childcare strategy document acknowledges that in order 'to meet the Government's vision, childcare must become part of partnership with parents to meet the cognitive, social, emotional and physical needs of children' (HM Treasury, DfES, DWP and DTI 2004).

Practitioners also acknowledge that, for babies, the first experience of life outside the home must be one in which the key people in their lives work together to create the conditions necessary for emotional health and resilience in order that they become strong, skilful, competent and healthy. The *Birth to Three Matters* framework, which supports practitioners working with young children, rests on the premise that parents matter to children: 'parents and families are central to the well being of the child' (DfES 2002). Yet for many practitioners their initial training has not equipped them to take on the important responsibility of working with and, in many cases, supporting parents and families. So in any vision for the future, practitioner support and training must be the highest priority.

Training matters

An issue acknowledged by the government is that the 'single biggest factor that determines the quality of childcare is the workforce' (HMT 2004: 44) and although the current workforce includes many capable and dedicated people, qualification levels remain low. This is compounded by the demand for additional childcare workers as increasing numbers of children's centres together with the varied contexts in which babies and young children are educated require staff with knowledge, skill, competence and confidence to meet the ever increasing demands of working in multidisciplinary teams and with professionals whose training will be quite different from their own.

Highlighting the important role played by a high-quality workforce a recent support document states:

> Effective practice in the early years requires committed, enthusiastic and reflective practitioners with a breadth and depth of knowledge, skill and understanding. Effective practitioners use their own learning to improve their work with young children and their families in ways which are sensitive, positive and non-judgemental.
>
> (DfES 2005a: 3)

The same document suggests that through initial, ongoing and continuous training and development practitioners need to develop, demonstrate and continuously improve their:

- relationships with both children and adults;
- understanding of the individual and diverse ways that children learn and develop;
- knowledge and understanding of ways to actively support and extend children's learning in and across all areas;
- practice in meeting all children's needs, learning styles and interests;
- work with parents, carers and the wider community;
- work with other professionals within and beyond the setting (DfES 2005a: 3).

Ways in which these necessary skills and understandings will be acquired are a major concern of the *Children's Workforce Strategy* (DfES 2005a), which is currently addressing the issue of what a common core of skills and knowledge will look like for practitioners working with children and families. While it could be argued that some of the other necessary skills identified in the *Common Core* document (DfES 2005b) could be applied to parents, the only ones that specifically mention parents are to 'Understand the role and value of families and carers as partners in supporting their children to achieve positive outcomes' (DfES 2005b: 8) and in relation to safeguarding and promoting the welfare of the child: 'To understand the key role of parents and carers in safeguarding and promoting children and young people's welfare and involve them accordingly, while recognising factors that can affect parenting and increase the risk of abuse' (DfES 2005b: 13).

Training needs to address ways in which new practitioners can acquire these skills. There are however some encouraging developments since as a central plank of UK government policy the notion of 'partnership' goes alongside an emphasis on 'user involvement' and 'user participation' in health and social care (Morrow and Malin 2004: 164). Opportunities to develop shared understandings are on the increase, particularly in the fields of health and social care, early childhood education, parenting education and work with families.

In an attempt to move away from the hierarchical connotations of the term 'parent involvement', Ball proposed a 'triangle of care' formed by parents, professionals and the community, with parents at the apex (1994: 45). The key to the success of this triangle of care was seen as the quality of the relationship between those involved. True partnership implies equality and a division of power that enables parents to take much more responsibility in relation to decision-making. Such a partnership might relate to their role in determining policy and influencing the day-to-day running of the out-of-home setting which plays such an important part in their own lives and that of their children in the years between birth and 3. On the other hand it could relate to the nature of the relationship that exists between parents and the many other professionals in a children's centre or Sure Start programme such as childminders, health visitors and social workers, although the degree to which real partnership has been achieved is debatable and such debates must guide future developments.

Morrow and Malin (2004) suggest that the notion of empowerment is often inherent in these debate. Empowerment is a term often used when considering parents' involvement. What we mean by empowerment with regard to parents, carers and practitioners is something which must continue to be addressed. Foot *et al.* (2002) suggest that while children's best interests have always been paramount in the notion of partnership between parents and professionals, views about the nature of that partnership have changed to a greater emphasis on the parents themselves as beneficiaries, a point emphasized by Margaret Henry in Chapter 4. In measuring how far we have come since Ball's insistence that professionals 'need to do more than pay lip-service to the idea that their relationship with parents is a partnership of equals' (1994: 46), Morrow and Malin (2004) refer to a study in which through 'involvement' and 'participation' in the design and working of a local Sure Start programme this notion of empowerment was achieved by encouraging practitioners to 'enable and empower parents and children to become more confident and self-reliant' (Ball 1994: 46). The study raises important issues for future debates and responses, not least the potential paradox of being a professional and being committed to empowerment. In considering this paradox Pease (2002) notes that part of the definition of a profession implies possession of a specific knowledge base, expertise and the holding of an institutional position that places professionals in a position of power over others. This raises further questions for debate, for example, how far in a multi-agency, interdisciplinary multi-professional world do early childhood practitioners represent a unified profession? Another question also arises: to what extent is the preparation of a new generation of professionals, trained through the *Common Core* (DfES 2005b), likely to be adequately prepared for working with parents and families? Comments, such as 'they don't make you feel stupid', 'you feel on the same level' and 'you're not seen as the problem but as part of the solution' are cited by Morrow and Malin as evidence that in their study parents were enabled to feel that they were active participants in the choices and decisions made with regard to parenting. The conclusions reached are that:

> Involvement in the Parents' Committee has clearly contributed to the 'personal empowerment' of its members, has provided parents with opportunities to build on their strengths and develop practical skills, to establish strong social networks and to create new relationships with professionals. At the same time, changing relationships and changing boundaries have implications for power relationships and for the identity of professionals and parents. For

those working in complex multi-agency settings this may cause tensions and dilemmas and present a challenge that has implications for support and training ...

(Morrow and Malin 2004: 175)

A new project designed to help practitioners cope with these kinds of challenges and dilemmas and also meet the demand for appropriate training in this field is the Parental Community Support Project 2005–2007. This consortium project run for the Sure Start Unit of the DfES by the National Children's Bureau (NCB), Coram Family and the London Borough of Camden identifies a number of key tasks and outputs. The first of these is the identification and dissemination of existing effective practice on parental support for children's learning as a basis for development of a core model on which to base a training course and materials to support practitioners in 500 communities which will include Sure Start local programmes, Early Excellence Centres and children's centres. Training will follow the model used in the *Birth to Three Matters* training with one day of supported self-study followed by one day of face-to-face training. Learning outcomes from the training will be mapped against two sets of national occupational standards and routes to accreditation will be identified. This ambitious and much-needed project will draw on and complement other current projects designed to support professionals in their work with parents. It will emulate the *Birth to Three Matters* project in that a thorough research and literature review will underpin the development of the core model.

As with the *Birth to Three Matters: A Review of the Literature* (David *et al.* 2003), this valuable review of research and materials will be published as a separate guide and disseminated more widely via the projects 'Rolling Resource', a feature of the NCB's Early Childhood Unit's website, www.early-childhood.org. The review will also be widely disseminated in other forms, via the partner organizations, the Sure Start website and through articles and news items. This kind of resource will allow for information specific to work with parents of babies and children under 3 to be available and for links with the single quality framework (DfES 2004), entitled the Early Years Foundation Stage (EYFS), to be made. The project's main emphasis will be on the role of parents in their children's learning and the identification of those practices and dispositions in both parents and practitioners which will lead to this kind of support. Existing work and experience within the field will be drawn upon in order to develop a training programme, which among other important issues, will examine the needs of parents with disabilities and of those from minority ethnic groups. There will be a clear mapping against the other processes in which trainees will be engaged – for example, quality assurance schemes and other qualifications.

The project will offer advice on how to cascade training and will be a significant development on two counts. The first in response to providing opportunities for accreditation in the light of concern that childcare workers are 'able to work constructively with parents' and the second that 'clearer and more accessible progression routes for the existing workforce' are required (HM Treasury, DfES, DWP and DTI 2004: 45). The project will also provide opportunities for training to address the specific needs of practitioners caring for and supporting babies and young children from birth to 3 and their families. The flexibility afforded by responsive projects such as this enables very specific issues such as supporting parents to be addressed. The original brief given to the *Birth to Three Matters* project team did not include specific consideration of the kinds of support for parents which the materials can offer. Evidence from parents of ways in which they have been helped and informed by using the *Birth to Three Matters* materials with practitioners is a clear indication that this kind of support should be included in the new Parental Community Support Project.

Recognition by the government that the quality of childcare is largely determined by the quality of the workforce has led to investment in significantly raising qualification levels and a recruitment campaign to increase and broaden the range of people entering the sector. While this commitment has important implications for initial training, the availability of continuing professional development for the existing workforce is essential. While there are heartening new developments and proposals to increase the range of courses, modules and training material, more appropriate training opportunities relating to parents and the birth to 3 age group are required for all practitioners. In particular, support for teachers working in children's centres whose initial training has not equipped them with the knowledge, skill or experience to work with this important age group and their parents is urgently required. Working with parents has been afforded very little time or attention generally in teacher education as the demands of a subject-driven curriculum have taken precedence. Specialization in working with very young children has often been seen as a 'dead end' where career prospects are concerned and students have been advised to 'keep their options open' by training to work with older children. This must change if the work, pay and conditions of service and hence the status of young children are to gain a higher profile.

A new professional qualification in working with parents offered by the Parents Centre at Coram Family will feed into and inform the Parental Community Support Project as it develops and rolls out. New National Occupational Standards (NOS) have been developed by the DfES and these are now the standards to which practitioners need to be trained and which should influence all new courses as they are being written. The Parenting Education and Support Forum (PESF) has produced the *Core Curriculum: Training for Work with Parents* (2004) as a means of training practitioners to the NOS. A six-unit accredited programme leading to a national qualification at Open College Network Level 2 or 3 aims to develop awareness about the needs of both parents and children and provide essential skills and knowledge for those who work with parents and families in a paid or voluntary capacity. New training units are being written as part of the Parenting Fund Project based on services which currently exist at Coram Family Services, around issues which have been highlighted by contributors to this book. These include work with adoptive parents and fathers, work with young parents and support for children's learning.

Leadership matters

Much depends upon the support and leadership provided to practitioners by the managers of the setting in which they are working and until recently leadership training has been non-existent. However, a new qualification seeks to redress the balance.

The lack of appropriately qualified and experienced staff to lead and manage the growing number of children's centres is currently being addressed via the introduction of a National Professional Qualification in Integrated Centre Leadership (NPQICL). This is the first national programme to address the need for leaders within a multi-agency early years setting. The qualification seeks to provide leaders and managers and emerging leaders and managers of integrated centres with an opportunity to create an ethos of community partnership working by coordinating coherent and seamless high-quality services for children and families. This much-needed programme supports the recommendations made in *Every Child Matters* (HM Treasury 2003). There are currently more than 170 integrated centres around the country with plans to expand this to 2500 by 2008 and 3500 by 2010, reinforcing the need for appropriately-qualified leaders and managers. Our vision of a future in which these centres are led by practitioners committed to working in partnership with parents and families can be realized via the NPQICL which aims specifically to support parents' understanding and involvement in the lives of their young children both in and out of the home.

New models of training

An innovative project based on five regional early childhood centres in England aims to identify training and support needs at a local level in relation to *Birth to Three Matters*. Funded by the Esmée Fairbairn Foundation and based at Manchester Metropolitan University, the project involves the appointment of a researcher/mentor, usually the centre head, together with an advanced skills practitioner in each of the five centres. Local training needs are addressed via focus and cluster groups, home visits, meetings with childminders, parents, preschools, private and voluntary sectors providers, health visitors and social workers. Centre-based and outreach training is provided and parent support groups and crèche facilities allow for childminders to attend training courses on a regular basis. With opportunities for accreditation and staff support in accessing further training, this model will allow parents and practitioners to access the 'climbing frame' model of qualifications. The model emphasizes the importance of locally-based training which meets community needs together with mentor support and access to a model of effective practice and integrated services. With the growing number of children's centres this is a model which could be replicated in each local authority in the future. But for it to work it would require adequate funding to be made available and further work on accreditation, links with awarding bodies, the involvement of local further education and higher education institutions and support at national and local levels. The model provides not only a vision for the future but evidence that when people work in partnership positive things can be achieved.

The *Children's Workforce Strategy* (DfES 2005a) aims at providing a 'world class workforce' and there is no doubt that major changes in training are required if this is to be achieved. Debate continues regarding the balance of graduate and non-graduate workers required, the issue of terminology, the concept of pedagogy, pay and conditions of service and the construction of and access to the qualifications 'climbing frame'. What is clear is that for practitioners at all levels and stages in their professional lives there are insufficient opportunities to study in depth, and at first hand, children's development and learning from birth to 3 and the implications for practitioners of working in partnership with parents and families.

Fortunately, there are 'pockets' of opportunity for students and practitioners to focus on these important areas at various levels of study, but these opportunities are far from universal. Working with Others in a Team, Parental Partnerships and Working with Other Professionals are units offered by the Council for Awards in Children's Care and Education (CACHE), the Open University and a number of higher education institutions across the country. The increasing number of Sector Endorsed Foundation Degrees and integrated degrees such as the Early Childhood Studies degree ensure that child development, birth to 3 and working with parents are given a high profile. However, opportunities for this kind of study remain limited, particularly for teachers who need to be fully equipped to work in children's centres or indeed any other setting in which babies, young children and their parents are found. In this respect their current training is woefully inadequate.

A revision of early years teacher education is urgently needed if the vision of a well-qualified workforce is to be realized. A rapid response to the shortage of appropriately-trained staff would be to quickly develop a new one-year Post Graduate Certificate of Education (PGCE) to be offered to graduates of integrated Early Childhood Studies degree programmes which provide a sound interdisciplinary training but currently do not qualify graduates to teach. This PGCE could be written by the Early Childhood Studies Degrees Network in direct response to the vision expressed in the Childcare Workforce Development Strategy and course content would include the key areas necessary for teachers working in multidisciplinary teams and in integrated centres. Thus common training could be offered nationally in colleges and universities by appropriately-qualified and experienced tutors.

Continuing professional development

For experienced teachers and other childcare staff, short courses covering child development with particular emphasis on the *Birth to Three Matters* framework, multi-professional awareness, working in partnership with parents, leadership and management, could be offered to meet the demands both of an expansion of children's centres and changes in response to new initiatives. Ring-fenced funding would be essential to ensure that course development, staff costs, including secondments and appropriate resourcing of new courses, were adequately covered. New projects such as Birth to Three Training Matters, described earlier, could be offered on a wider scale and, together with expansion at national level of new initiatives currently taking place on a regional and local basis, significant change could result. Tried and tested programmes such as the Peers Early Education Partnership (PEEP) project and newer initiatives such as the Parental Community Support Project among others are already meeting with success, but programmes such as these tend to be locally-based and have relied on funding from charitable bodies and other agencies. In order to guarantee their continuation and expansion nationally as part of a continuing professional development programme, government funding and commitment would be necessary.

The success of the PEEP programme has much to do with the central role afforded to parents and the support offered to them in interacting with their babies and young children. Set up in a disadvantaged area of Oxford in 1985, PEEP aims to promote educational achievement, especially literacy, and views positive self-esteem and the disposition to learn as essential preconditions for successful learning. Weekly group sessions enable parents to get to know each other, and to work with experienced practitioners enjoying listening, talking, singing and playing with their own and with other children. PEEP recognizes the rapid rate of very early learning and acknowledges and celebrates parents as the child's first educators. Provision of resources for use at home, access to a well-stocked toy library, home visits and group involvement support parents in developing skill and confidence in themselves and in their role as educator. Training has taken place in other parts of the country and what began on one housing estate in Oxford is now successfully replicated in many different areas. The opportunity for accreditation for those parents completing the programme and recognition of achievement in ways that contribute towards a qualification are also important incentives in the present climate.

The findings of a major longitudinal evaluation study of the PEEP programme, the *Birth to School Study* (Evangelou *et al.* 2005) contribute to the existing body of evidence on the efficacy of early interventions with strong parental involvement. The study has important implications for policy – firstly, for the continued funding of those early interventions that have strong parental partnerships; and secondly for the expansion of the provision of such interventions. Centre-based programmes are clearly meeting local needs. Parents around the country are providing evidence that a good relationship with their children's carers and involvement in their children's early learning is benefiting them as well as their children.

Dissemination of effective practice and sharing ideas with a view to replication in other centres is an aim of the *Foundation Stage Parents* pilot project (DfES 2005c), which involves seven local authorities, chosen to illustrate a range of ways of responding to the diversity in communities, settings and families. Learning stories are shared in accessible leaflet format. Each of the seven projects is quite different in its aims and focus. For example, the Northumberland Healthy Pathway Award supports early years settings in the process of supporting parents in their child's education by raising awareness of health-related issues and their impact on learning. It represents a partnership between health and education and recognizes the need for whole-community involvement in providing a stimulating physical and social environment.

The Camden Developing Partnerships with Parents and Practitioners: Planning for Play Together project involves parents as partners and active participants empowered by knowledge and involvement in observing and analysing their child's play. A loan scheme of treasure boxes for use in the home together with regular discussion and reflection with practitioners helps to build a picture of how practitioner behaviour influences the type of dialogue they have with parents.

The Wakefield Families Enjoying Everything Together (FEET) project supports families with 2- and 3-year-old children and involves parents, practitioners and children enjoying playing and learning together for two terms prior to admission into the Foundation Stage. The programme has succeeded in increasing confidence and raising self-esteem in both parents, practitioners and children and will be introduced more widely as children's centres are developed.

In Gloucestershire, the Foundation Stage Parent Partnership Project builds on a well-established family learning programme which aims to increase skills, confidence and attitudes to learning. Materials emphasizing the importance of play-based learning will be developed in modular format with opportunities for accreditation for parents and practitioners.

In Newcastle upon Tyne, the Helping Your Child to Learn programme has been set up to support parents and carers to learn more about themselves and their children through exploring the principles and philosophy of the University of the First Age, dedicated to transforming teaching and learning for children and their families through the creation of an environment in which everyone feels emotionally safe and sufficiently confident to take risks with their learning. The programme emphasizes the importance of language, diet and nutrition, and sensory stimulation, which includes baby massage and movement in learning. The approach was originally pioneered in Birmingham and now works in partnership with 32 local authorities across England.

In Norfolk the Adventures in Play programme works through a multi-professional network of providers, parents and practitioners sharing in a range of workshop activities based on a variety of role-play scenarios. A series of role-play boxes on loan help parents to engage with their children in this kind of activity at home and video materials support parents' understanding of the importance of play in young children's learning. An adviser, link teacher or advanced skills practitioner is available to support and lead workshops.

The Peterborough Parents and Professionals Raising Aspirations Together project aims to strengthen links between home and school in order to build confidence, self-esteem and a deeper understanding of play for all children and their families. Parents observe and record their children at play, involving video and photographs of home and out-of-home activities, and these are then analysed and discussed with practitioners. A dissemination conference provides an opportunity for sharing effective practice with other authorities, practitioners and parents.

The DfES *Engaging Fathers* project (2004) highlights the importance of involving fathers in their children's learning and aims to identify the sort of programmes and activities that attract them. Findings indicate that when invitations are targeted at fathers, and father/child activities in particular, and not labelled for 'parents', fathers are more likely to respond. Where staff welcome and consult fathers about content, timing and recruitment, making them feel comfortable about their inclusion, they are more positive about being involved.

As Tricia David indicates in Chapter 3, grandparents play a vital role in supporting parents of babies and young children, and children themselves. The report *Grandparents Talking* (2003), by the charity Grandparents Plus, calls for greater government recognition and debate about the vital caring role that grandparents can provide. Equally, support for practitioners in working in partnership with the wider family unit is needed.

Thus while there remains much to do before we can fully claim on behalf of all local authorities, early years settings and practitioners that 'parents really do matter', there is nevertheless much to celebrate. Government commitment, innovative and challenging projects, children's workforce developments and a wealth of research evidence bear witness to the fact that work will continue in order to realize the vision in which practitioners are fully prepared to support the varying needs of children, parents and families and to work in true partnership with the home – a partnership that recognizes that skilful thinking, effective communication and emotional health and well-being develop out of shared experiences for parents and practitioners as well as children.

References

Ball, C. (1994) *Start Right: The Importance of Early Learning*. London: Royal Society for the Encouragement of the Arts, Manufacturers and Commerce (RSA).

David, T., Gough, K., Powell, S. and Abbott, L. (2003) *Birth to Three Matters: A Review of the Literature*. London: DfES Publications.

DfES (2002) *Birth to Three Matters*. London: DfES Publications.

DfES (2003) *Every Child Matters: Change for Children*. London: DfES Publications.

DfES (2004) *Engaging Fathers: Involving Parents, Raising Achievement*. London: DfES Publications.

DfES (2005a) *Children's Workforce Strategy: A Strategy to Build a World Class Workforce for Children and Young People*. London: DfES Publications.

DfES (2005b) *Common Core of Skills and Knowledge for the Children's Workforce: Every Child Matters, Change for Children*. London: DfES Publications.

DfES (2005c) *Foundation Stage Parents, Partners in Learning: Primary National Strategy*. London: DfES Publications.

Evangelou, M., Brooks, G., Smith, S. and Jennings, D. (2005) *The Birth to School Study: A Longitudinal Evaluation of the Peers Early Education Partnership (PEEP) (1998–2005)*. London: DfES Publications.

Foot, H. *et al.* (2002) Parental participation and partnership in pre-school provision, *International Journal of Early Years Education*, 10(1): 5–18.

Grandparents Plus (2003) *Grandparents Talking: Report of Seminar Held at the Nuffield Foundation, London, 5 June 2005*. London: Grandparents Plus.

HM Treasury, DfES, DWP and DTI (2004) *Choice for Parents, the Best Start for Children: A Ten Year Strategy*. London: HM Treasury.

Morrow, G. and Malin, N. (2004) Parents and professionals working together: turning the rhetoric into reality, *Early Years*, 1(2): 175.

Parenting Education and Support Forum (2004) *Core Curriculum: Training for Work with Parents*. London: Parenting Education and Support Forum.

Pease, B. (2002) Rethinking empowerment: a postmodern reappraisal for emancipating practice, *British Journal of Social Work*, 32(2): 135–47.

Pugh, G. (1999) Young children and their families: creating a community response, in L. Abbott and H. Moylett (eds) *Early Education Transformed*. Buckingham: Open University Press.

Vandevelde, M. (2000) Planetary Influences, in L. Abbott and H. Moylett (eds) *Early Education Transformed*. Buckingham: Open University Press.

Index